Competing
for Capital

John Wiley & Sons

Founded in 1807, John Wiley & Sons is the oldest independent publishing company in the United States. With offices in North America, Europe, Australia, and Asia, Wiley is globally committed to developing and marketing print and electronic products and services for our customers' professional and personal knowledge and understanding.

The Wiley Finance series contains books written specifically for finance and investment professionals as well as sophisticated individual investors and their financial advisors. Book topics range from portfolio management to e-commerce, risk management, financial engineering, valuation and financial instrument analysis, as well as much more.

For a list of available titles, visit our Web site at www.WileyFinance.com.

Competing for Capital

*Investor Relations
in a Dynamic World*

BRUCE W. MARCUS

WILEY

John Wiley & Sons, Inc.

To my wife, Mana
You make it worthwhile doing

Contents

Acknowledgments

There is a myth that individuals invent things. Robert Fulton and his paddle boat. James Watt and the steam engine. Edison and his light bulb. The Wright brothers and the airplane.

It's a myth, all right. Before each of these people produced a useable machine, a lot of scientists and thinkers and dreamers (and maybe alchemists) started the process that culminated in the inventor's invention.

The same, I can tell you, is true of books. We writers toil alone, like monks illuminating manuscripts, pounding at our keyboards and growling at the intrusions of the outside world (and our wives, of course), and in danger of thinking that just because our names are on the book jackets, we did it alone. Never in a million years.

Every concept in this book (and in every other book I've written) has been vetted by my experience—I'm not an academic, I write from my own experience—except, of course, for most of the new regulatory material. I'm not a lawyer. And except, also, for the input, and critiques and contributions and suggestions of my very wise friends. This is their book as well as mine, and I'm grateful to them beyond words.

Dixie Waterson, my once and forever colleague and friend, gave me the first list of suggestions. She is a consummate investor relations professional, and if she were older, she'd be a Grand Dame of the profession.

Lou Thompson, the president of NIRI, and his staff, was generous beyond words in keeping me up to date on regulations and techniques. The information prodigiously produced by NIRI for its members informed much of this book. No profession has a greater champion, nor a greater organization to lean on for professional wisdom.

My old friend and one-time client, Bill Donaldson, is now the head of the SEC. For appropriate reasons, he contributed nothing to this book, nor has he seen a word of it prior to completion. But he did supply two things—encouragement, and a revolution in the financial world to write about. Wall Street—and Main Street—will never be the same after his tenure, but will be better for it.

Richard Levick and Larry Smith, of Boston-based Levick Strategic Communications, LLP, are the leading practitioners of law firm marketing, and media relations, and kept me up to speed on the rapidly changing media picture. And so too did my old and dear friend, Jennifer Prosek, of New York and Stratford CT-based Cubitt, Jacobs & Prosek, who has built a mighty international publicity machine from a small operation in rural Connecticut. She has been unsparing of her time, in the use of the facilities of her firm, in the time and help of her own investor relations staff, and in her own wisdom. Her overseas partner, Mark Kollar, and Katie Vusak of her office, helped fill in some blanks from their own investor relations clientele.

I've known Jeff Corbin's father for eons, and he was a great public relations and investor relations consultant for years. Now Jeff runs the firm—KCSA—and he's built it into the world's largest independent investor relations firm. Jeff, whose knowledge of this field is formidable, gave me time and help.

I was overwhelmed by Donna Brooks, of the Hartford-based law firm, Shipman & Goodwin. She supplied expertise and her practical experience on Sarbanes-Oxley and the SEC, and then took a lawyer's pen to the draft of the chapter on regulation. This is more than a generosity of time and wisdom—it's a generosity of spirit. Jim Schulwolf, my friend and her partner, was particularly helpful with ideas and references.

June Filingeri, president of Comm-Partners LLC, who practices the investor relations art from a small town in Connecticut with big city skills, contributed her ideas, her knowledge, her challenges to my ideas, and her support.

My children, Lucy and David, were my coauthors on two parts of the book. Lucy, based in England (and the whole world, its seems), is a consultant to the financial community. Her firm is Marcus Venture Consulting (www.marcusventures.com). She contributed her widely used guidelines to writing a business plan for seekers of capital in the world's capital markets.

David, a venture capitalist, is Managing Director, Life Sciences, at Boston-based VIMAC Ventures. He brought me up to speed on what the venture capitalists are doing these days, and wrote those paragraphs for this book. A wise and good son.

At those times when an author's brains go numb, he needs the conversation and enthusiastic support of a few bright people. That role in my life is inevitably played by Patrick McKenna and Gerry Riskin, the world's (yes, the world's) leading consultants to law firms. Patrick lives in Edmonton, Canada and Gerry lives in Anguilla, but they are ubiquitous, and rarely in the same place at the same time. The one place they are always in together is in my heart and mind. Thanks for that.

Research, when you live in a small town in Connecticut, ain't easy. That's why I cherish the Libraries in Easton and Trumbull. I worked my way through college (it was medieval times, I think) in the Brooklyn Public Library, in Brooklyn, New York, and I know the mettle of librarians. That's why I cherish the likes of Easton's head librarian, Bernadette Baldino, and the magician of the EPL computer, Penelope Papadoulis, as well as the patient, helpful and always accommodating staff at the Trumbull library. Thank you ladies and gentlemen.

Kathryn Davis, a dear friend, has long since surpassed the record I once held for the number of annual reports I wrote. Believe me, she was helpful. As was Scott Greenberg, who heads the remarkable Curren & Conners, certainly the leading producers of corporate annual reports and other material for the financial community. He gave me his valuable input on the trends in the field. He knows, and he's the best at what the knows.

August Aquila and I go back many years in the professional services marketing field, and so it was natural that he and I should write the ultimate book on marketing professional services—*Client At the Core*, also published by Wiley in 2004. He is a good and knowledgeable friend, and a patient one at that.

And as ever, my friend and mentor, Richard Weiner. He knows, and he taught me what he knows.

As the author of many books, I know full well the tensions that arise between publishers and authors. But for more than 20 years, and through two publishing houses, Pamela van Giessen has been my publisher, my muse, my task master, and the patient and gentle guide to quite a few of my books. She prods, appropriately, but never nags. She gets it done. As a writer, I'd follow her anywhere. And she always has assistants who give surrogate a good name. Jennifer McDonald, in this case, helped bring this book to your hands.

As for the good lady Mana, my wife of more than 40 years, there are not enough words of praise and gratitude in the language equal to the task of describing her. I think it must be easier to be a coal miner's wife than the wife of a writer. She could give lessons. She is a muse above all others, and will be for the writing to come.

There are, of course, others. But the list would be longer than the book itself. To all of you, my eternal gratitude.

This book descends from my first book, also *Competing For Capital*, published in 1975, and *Competing For Capital in the '80s*, published in 1982. It's amazing the changes that have been wrought in the intervening years. It's amazing what's stayed the same. If you've read any of these books, you'll find some of this vaguely familiar. The vagary comes from change in the world of investor relations.

Readers of my books on marketing, and my online newsletter, *The Marcus Letter on Professional Services Marketing* (www.marcusletter.com), will find the basic marketing principles familiar as well. They're principles I've been espousing for years, in books and innumerable articles.

And so, this is more than my book—it's *our* book. I'm lucky to know and to have the help and guidance of friends like these. Who says writing isn't luck?

Bruce W. Marcus

Preface

To ignore history, said the philosopher Santayana, is to doom oneself to repeat the past. Go tell that to the investment community, and those who serve it.

In 1975, when the first edition of *Competing for Capital* was written, we lived in an era in which I said that three chestnut venders could meet, greet one another cordially, and then go public. We called that time in history the *go-go years*, when the small investor and the large institution alike discovered the great investing game as a year-round sport. Companies were going public at breakneck pace, the institutions were growing at breakneck pace, and the small investor was learning to read the ticker tape. Corporate America, steeped in the tradition of privacy and shutting out the general public, began to see the advantage of opening its books to attract investors, thereby breeding the new practice we now call investor relations. It was an era of a new populism in the stock market, fed by hope, by great stories in new companies, and by unbridled optimism.

It was a time, too, when financial publications were read mostly by investment professionals, when business news in popular media was relegated to the obscure corners and reported by reporters with little or no financial background, and when new communications vehicles (PR Newswire, for example) were emerging. And of course, there were no computers. Investing was in. Basic investment principles were out in this new game of investing and raising capital.

When the bubble burst in 1987, and the market took a nosedive, the sobering effect on the investment community, and particularly the individual investor, was a promise of "never again." Never again would the public be taken in by such irrational exuberance (familiar phrase?). Never again would the people's capitalism be tainted by such greed and gullibility.

We can laugh about that now. The exuberance of the 1990's, fed by the new world of technology and its producers, far exceeded that of the *go-go years*. We talked of a new economy, a new breed of investors, a new kind of economic sophistication in which a small investment could be parlayed into a vast fortune almost overnight. We talked of a new music we could dance to until dawn without growing weary.

New investment vehicles, new forms and sources of data transmittal and other uses of a new technology, a proliferating business and investment media, the 401(k) retirement investment vehicle, the glamorous new stars of industry, and a new generations of investors and investment professionals (perhaps too young to remember the go-go years)—all created a new climate for the end of the century. The Dow Jones Average, a comfortable 3000 in 1975, reached more than 12,000 in 1999, and then, following the dot com disaster, fell again to around 10,000. By 2004, it was still hovering around 10,000, but not comfortably.

Participation of individual investors is changing. More than 50% of Americans now hold stocks, not only as individual investors, but through corporate retirement funds, mutual funds and straight out purchase.

It also produced a massive greed that inevitably generated bold and pervasive corruption, and an epidemic bending, breaking, ignoring rules. Ingenious corporate officers who knew how to amass fortunes at the expense of investors and employees. Accountants, the guardians of the public interest, so immersed in the greediness of their clients that they broke tablet after tablet of the auditor's commandments to protect the interest of the investor. Vast corporate investment in political life corrupted law makers. "It's not that humans have become any more greedy than in generations past," said Alan Greenspan, chairman of the Federal Reserve Bank. "It is that the venues to express greed had grown so enormously."

In the best traditions of greed, day traders—investors who jumped in and out of the market in a single day to take advantage of incremental market movements—warped the market itself, diminishing its orderliness. The daily volume of stock trading burgeoned, and where once a price/earnings ratio of 14 to 18 was considered responsible, stock prices were being run up by a greed-driven market to price/earnings ratios in the hundreds, as blind optimism trumped reality.

And then, once again, the bubble burst. So many of those wonderful dot com companies that we believed were perpetual fountains of unlimited wealth fell apart, and proved to be glitter on the outside and hollow on the inside. An astonishing number of CEOs, whose salaries and bonuses and stock options reached outlandish ratios to the salaries of their employees, turned out to be authors of outrageous frauds. Enron. WorldCom. HealthSouth. Tyco. And all aided by the greed of auditors, who seemed willing to subvert the independence of their invaluable attest function in order to accumulate more revenue from their clients. Then there was the corruption of the brokers and security analysts who knowingly lied to the public about the quality of the stocks they touted, because their firms had financed those companies, and the analysts didn't want to shut the fountain of new investment business from their investment banking clients.

It's not the purpose of this book to assess the reasons for this rash of skullduggery, other than to note that greed is greed, mendacity is mendacity, and stupidity is stupidity, and arrogance is bred of greed and mendacity and stupidity. The events speak for themselves.

The years 2001 and 2002 saw a reaction by the public, the investment community, the White House, Congress, the regulatory agencies, and the rule making bodies of the various professions involved in making and monitoring the rules governing their professions. The optimism of the last decade changed to skepticism, fear, anxiety and a loss of faith in the integrity of the very organizations supposed to protect investors. Suddenly, the face of capitalism changed, and is continuing to change.

In fact, the regulatory changes brought about by Sarbanes-Oxley, and by a newly energized and empowered Securities and Exchange Commission, are causing a revolution in American capitalism. Responsibility for corporate financial helmsmanship moves more and more from the CEO and CFO to the board of directors. The rules have changed, and corporate governance will never again be as they were in the 20th century.

Nor will the professions be the same. New accounting firm and auditing regulations mean new ways—and new responsibilities—to deal with old reporting problems may radically change traditional accounting firm structures and practices. Note that the once Big Eight is now the Big Four, not only by merger of the giants, but by the demise of the once-great Arthur Andersen.

Law firms, too, face new real and potential changes, with challenges to their responsibilities to clients and to traditional client confidentiality rules.

All in all, it's a new economic environment in which the corporate world must function.

So too is the practice of investor relations changing, and changing radically. New rules. New problems in projecting investment values and the integrity of corporate management and corporate information. New problems in separating the political from the financial reality. New problems in knowledge management. New sources of data, and data that proliferates at an overwhelming rate. New technology to speed data, if not wisdom, to target audiences. The growth of internationalism, bringing us closer to one world than ever before.

When I first started in this business, more than 40 years ago. We didn't call it investor relations. It was financial public relations—public relations, but to a financial community. The first investor relations practitioners were actually public relations practitioners, usually with the merest smattering of understanding of finances and investment principles. Gradually recognizing the advantages of financial knowledge, a few firms started hiring some out of work security analysts. A few of us went back to school to learn how to read a balance sheet and other financial arts. Ultimately, as the investment world matured, and reached out in many ways to a growing investment public, financial public relations grew to become investor relations, and the financial public relations practitioner became the investment relations officer.

The investment relations officer has long since been a fully trained financial professional, who uses communications skills to impart the values of the company to an investment public. The organization serving the investor relations professional—The National Investor Relations Institute (NIRI)—is as valuable to its members and the profession it serves as any professional body, including the American Bar Association and the American Institute of Certified Public Accountants. NIRI sustains the professionalism of its members, informs and educates them, and fosters their integrity. NIRI membership is now in excess of 4,400.

NIRI defines investor relations as "...a strategic management responsibility that integrates finance, communication, marketing, and securities law compliance to enable the most effective two-way communication between a company, the financial community, and other constituencies, which ultimately contributes to a company's securities achieving fair valuations."

I concur. But in 1975, in the first edition of this book, I defined the process as a form of competing for capital in a highly competitive capital market. This is still the case, except that in view of the events of the first years of the 21st century, the rules have changed substantially, as have the participants and the vehicles of communications to the investment public. How to do it—how to think about it—in this decade, in a new and tumultuous environment, is what this book is about.

Bruce W. Marcus
Easton, CT, August 1, 2004

Competing
for Capital

CHAPTER 1

Strategic Factors in a New Environment

The Coming of Sarbanes-Oxley and the Brave New World

In the few months at the end of 2001 and the beginning of 2002, the corporate and financial world saw the beginnings of a revolution of a magnitude not seen since the 1930s. Reports of corporate fraud in major companies burst like fireworks in a Summer sky. Long established concepts of prudence and integrity in financial reporting were shown to have eroded to a degree that not only surprised and shocked the investment community, but caused the downfall of a great many prominent and once-admired corporate leaders. The number of giant companies and great corporate names revealed to be rotten at the core began to be double digit. Perhaps most shocking, because it had been the icon for integrity and probity for so many generations, was the destruction of the auditing and accounting firm Arthur Andersen, once the leading and most respected name in the accounting profession. Andersen had, it seems, been derelict in too many of its audits, and was found to have been at least asleep as client fraud paraded by. The firm had possibly been a participant in the fraud at some level.

Not surprisingly, investor confidence sank to new lows. The stock market, already suffering from the burst bubble of the dot com failures, dropped precipitously. If the financial information coming from such giants as Enron, WorldCom, Tyco, HealthSouth and many, many others was so flagrantly and dishonestly reported to investors, how could an investor trust the numbers and other information coming from any other corporation, no matter how big, no matter how well respected? If numbers given to the government and investors from such companies as these and others too numerous to list had to be restated, how could an investor know which corporate numbers could be trusted?

If Big Four accounting firms, the bastions of independence, could be sued for one or more careless or faulty audits, where are the concepts of integrity in the attest function that once gave comfort to both management and investors?

Where were the monitors—those who were supposed to protect the investor? The U.S. Securities and Exchange Commission, overwhelmed, under-funded, restrained by Washington politics, had neither the teeth nor the manpower to do what they knew had to be done, nor the support of congress to enforce the SEC's mandate. The New York Stock Exchange, whose traditional structures had barely changed in the decades in which a vast array of business and economic changes had transpired, was caught in a management maelstrom that toppled its leadership.

For decades, the accounting profession had fought repeated attempts to have the accountants give self-regulation over to an outside governmental body. The American Institute of Certified Public Accountants—the AICPA—continued to the last minute to insist that only the accounting profession had the knowledge and wherewithal to set accounting standards and to uphold the integrity of those who audited financial statements. But then the events of this business revolution clearly showed them to be incapable of any real control over the integrity of the attest function.

On Wall Street, the presumed independence of security analysts and others who supply investment advice to shareholders was shown to be a farce in a great many quarters. Analysts with security underwriting firms were found to be giving false positive recommendations on securities underwritten by their own firms. It was a scandal that led to indictments of prominent names on Wall Street.

In his book, *The Future of Freedom,* Fareed Zakaria, the editor of *Newsweek International,* says that professionals (accountants, lawyers, investment bankers, and even doctors) have turned their backs on their traditional responsibilities to protect and guide the individuals they serve. The chicanery epidemic was no longer a secret.

And so, the increasing anxiety of a vast number of investors, both institutional and individual, and their growing skepticism about the information supplied by corporations and certified by auditors, and the diminished value and integrity of brokers and analysts, caused a cry and an outrage — a demand that the government do something.

It did. The Sarbanes-Oxley Act of 2002.

SARBANES-OXLEY TO THE RESCUE

In one grand stroke, the Act put greater controls on corporate governance, on the oversight of the accounting profession, and on the independence of security analysts. The U.S. Securities and Exchange Commission, long overwhelmed by the venue it served, was given new teeth, and the funds to do its job effectively.

The law strengthened the audit committee of the board of directors, giving it powers that it either never had before, or had, but ignored. No longer an audit committee in name only, often comprised of the CEO's cronies, the law now demands financial expertise of its members. It has new responsibilities in selecting and monitoring the outside auditors and on internal audit controls. The audit committee is, under the new law, freed from subservience to the corporation's management. This represents a major shift in traditional corporate governance. Ultimately, it guards the shareholder's equity from the whims of a strong executive and a weak board.

CEO's and CFO's now have responsibility to sign off on the accuracy of the corporations' quarterly and annual financial statements. To certify falsely, or to certify statements that don't conform to Sarbanes-Oxley, can mean as much as $5 million and 20 year's in jail, or both.

Greater regulation of brokerage firms, security analysts, and sources of capital substantially alter the structure and management of financial institutions. The new rules separate stock analysts from the investment bankers, eliminating the practice of analysts recommending stocks of poor quality because the investment banking side was the underwriter.

These are real laws that dictate strong civil and criminal punishments for violations, and not just rhetoric. Although not perfect solutions, the greater controls on corporate boards and audit committees alter the very nature of corporate governance.

Stronger controls on auditors were instigated, including separation of auditing and consulting practices and reexamining partnership structures, shift the burden of integrity from within the practice to outside bodies. Self-regulation is out. Oversight is in.

Significantly, the law took oversight of auditing rules away from the accounting profession and gave that responsibility to a newly created Public Company Accounting Oversight Board—the PCAOB.

New SEC regulations, such as Regulation FD (for Fair Disclosure), redefined the rules of disclosure, and were strengthened with new enforcement actions against companies in violation of its dictates.

There is an irony here. Not too many years ago, many corporations insisted on their right to limit the information given to shareholders. In the 1950s, the major role of many investor relations professionals was to stand outside the board room, waiting for permission to release the dividend announcement or quarterly reports. Many corporations fought with sharp talons any attempt to peek inside the corporate suite. Those were the days when investor relations was still called financial public relations, and most financial relations practitioners were public relations people with little or no financial background.

Subsequent government and exchange regulations, and the growth of stock ownership, caused corporations to recognize that what we now call investor relations was crucial to compete successfully in the capital markets. Wooing investors in a growing economy became more intense, and with the help of one of the most useful and successful associations in both the financial and communications world, NIRI—the National Investor Relations Institute—investor relations became a highly professional practice.

To better understand the foundations of the new economic environment, the new breeding ground of both good and bad events of the beginning of the 21st century, we need only look at the changes in the business world, and the role of the new technology.

In the course of the last quarter of the 20th Century, a number of factors converged to radically change the economic environment in which the corporation and the investor functioned. These changes affected, as well, the art and practice of investor relations, and thereby the visibility of the corporation to the investing public.

We've seen the increasing importance of the internet in all aspects of communication—to shareholders, analysts and other influentials in the investment community. The business and financial media, aided by the internet, redefine the access to information by investors, and bring a new dimension in investment theory. The internet is now entrenched as an integral part of the corporate information channel.

An expanded business and financial press, with new business media, further redefined the access to information by investors. This access to an overwhelming abundance of data and online databases, and the new dimension it brings to investment information, brings, as well, new problems in managing the data for value, effectiveness, and communication, with investors given more information than they ever had before—but without meaningful interpretation. Consolidations of sources of data and external communications control the flow of information through new structures and alliances.

This new and rapid dissemination of readily accessible information changes the nature of the information itself as it's accessed.

First, more people have access to the same information than ever before. Their decisions to act on it, or to choose not to act on it, alters the meaning of the information, at least by changing the effect of that action or non-action. And the greater the number of people who have access to the information, the greater the magnitude of the change. A simple example is the way the price of a stock will drop on good news, rather than rise, as would seem obvious.

Second, more extensive business and financial news is available online, on radio and television, and in the press—making investment decisions seem easier to make—but not always.

Then there is the growing number of investors. The 401(k) investment plans bring a bounty of new investors, but too often they are inexperienced and unsophisticated, and frequently alter an orderly market through irrational investment decisions.

To add to the mix, the economy went into decline at the turn of the 21st century, and then took almost four years to show just a glimpse of recovery. The rapid disintegration of the budget surplus, and the subsequent record deficit didn't help, either. It may be a decade more before we can assess the cost of the war on terrorism, and the effects of the invasion and occupation of Iraq.

With the burgeoning of the new world of technology in the 1980s and 1990s, and the fiscal discipline of the Clinton Administration and its astute Secretary of the Treasury, Robert Rubin, the country went through a period of extraordinary growth and prosperity. A shrewd Federal Reserve Bank leadership helped. The country's wealth, both corporate and individual, ballooned. The administration that followed brought in its own conservative economic theories, including massive tax cuts, and the economy took a 180 degree turn. The budget surplus quickly turned into a deficit.

To feed the needs of a capital hungry economy, the 1930's Glass-Steagal Act, which kept commercial banks out of the equities market, was allowed to die, first by attrition, and then by repeal. The country was in a capital bacchanal.

But consequently, optimism outpaced reality. Many companies, particularly in the high tech industry, became vehicles for entrepreneurs more interested in building personal stock market wealth than in addressing the realities of the marketplace. Venture capitalists and investment bankers misplaced their traditional prudence and knowledge of investment basics. The IPO—Initial Public Offering—became a game in which, as the author Adam Smith (George Goodman) put it, money was just the way we kept score. Price/earnings ratios, the stock market's measure of investment optimism, went so high on the pressure gauge that explosion was inevitable. And then the inevitable happened.

BEN GRAHAM IS RIGHT AGAIN

The basic principles, such as those delineated by Benjamin Graham in his classic book, *The Stock Market,* ignored by the accumulators of stock market wealth, turned out to be right. The market plunged as inflated stocks exploded. The investment landscape changed, virtually overnight.

This capital market frenzy was aided by a number of circumstances that changed the nature of corporate communications, and therefore, investor relations as well.

This new economic configuration greeted the country at the beginning of this century. The economy faced not just the failure of high tech companies whose stock had been inflated beyond any sense of reality, but the inability of a new administration in Washington to stem the excess that led to that failure. At a time when we needed further investment in the economy, and a greater degree of investor confidence, we faced war. First Afghanistan, then Iraq. Then came tax cuts that failed to bolster an eroding economy beyond a short economic spurt. A vast budget surplus turned into an overwhelming deficit, which can feed the economic downturn, and ultimately, breed inflation. There are reminders of the period during the Vietnam conflict, when the administration fought an expensive war without increasing taxes to pay for it. The subsequent inflation then was in the double digits. The cost of the war on terrorism, the invasion of Iraq, and the post war expenses to run each of these countries until they were able to develop oil revenues and a political economy in which they governed themselves, contributed to substantially altering the economic landscape.

Where once investor relations was considered to be merely ancillary to corporate and investment management, it now becomes a major corporate responsibility in generating trust and understanding in a highly competitive investment community.

Where once the emphasis of investor relations was on informing the investor and those who advise investors, that emphasis has shifted to the need to project accuracy and integrity. This, obviously, is much harder than merely reporting the numbers and other corporate values. Trust and integrity are abstractions that must be demonstrated, not merely espoused.

These factors, separately and together, dictate new strategies in informing and persuading investors, and those who advise them, of the values inherent in investing in a company's securities.

In many respects, Sarbanes-Oxley and the enforcement of Regulation FD redefine the practice of investor relations.

The new rules are clear, and redefine the practice of investor relations as never before. After decades of vaguery about the rules of disclosure, those rules, too, are now clearer, if not totally so.

The challenge of projecting the integrity of the company becomes easier, if you realize that Sarbanes-Oxley is really about the investor. By conforming to the rules of Sarbanes-Oxley, and then projecting that conformity, the investor is put at ease. How? Any number of ways, from putting a panel describing the new structure of the audit committee in an annual or quarterly report, by sending a media release about the audit committee, by focusing on conformity to both the press and the investment community.

It's obviously a new world for investor relations practitioners. Sarbanes-Oxley, the new stringency of the SEC, the new demands of the investor—all these and more define a fertile ground for effective investor relations.

And if this new regulatory environment causes us to pay attention to making our gardens grow, how do we best cultivate it? What are the strategies to best help companies compete for capital in this new environment? Read on.

CHAPTER 2

The New Investor— and What Influences the Investment Decision

This Ain't Your Father's House No More

It's fashionable to say that things have changed. Of course they have. Things are always changing.

But picture a blue collar worker, sitting in front of a computer in his den, checking the stocks in his 401k portfolio, and you begin to sense the reality of change in the investment world.

Picture stock trades made around the world on the internet, regardless of the place of origin. If capital has long known no borders, it now knows no time limits, as trades are made globally at lightning speed, unlimited by opening or closing bells.

Consider the availability of company information on the internet— information in vast quantities, virtually in real time, accessible to anybody, any day, any time.

And all of this in a regulatory environment that substantially alters corporate governance.

This is not, to paraphrase an old advertising slogan, your father's investor, nor your father's stock market, nor—for all that and all that— your father's technology. And it certainly isn't your father's regulatory environment. It clearly isn't your father's investor relations marketplace.

But marketplace it certainly is, and a highly competitive one at that.

The skills and techniques for reading and defining that marketplace— the art and science of investor relations—seem to have come fully into maturity in the last few years—at the end of the 20th century and the beginning of the 21st century. Any number of factors account for it. The extraordinary work of NIRI helped turn a random set of investor relations skills into a major profession. The growing intensity of competing for capital, especially to serve the new classes of investors, certainly bred new skills, as wars foster new medical discoveries. Technology, and the ability to move not only capital more rapidly than ever before, but information as well. The new technology has altered not only the way both corporations and those who invest, but our lives as well.

The prophetic Ted Pincus, founder and retired chairman of The Financial Relations Board, was right when he said, in an interview in the *Wall Street Journal* in 1996, that, "When the history of the 20th century stock market is written, scholars may well identify the openness and candor of modern-day corporate communications as a key factor in renewing and building investor confidence—ultimately leading to the amazingly sustainable buoyancy of the equity market in the '90s." To which might be added that when the market fell following the dot com failures, and began to rise again in recovery, it was those companies with professional investor relations professionals that best sustained.

Note, too, that he said it at a time that was not too distant from an era on Wall Street that had been characterized by decades of reticence by corporate leadership to tell anybody much of anything. That was in 1996, and it still holds true.

The year 2002 was characterized by the anxious wringing of well-manicured hands. It was the season of fraud and chicanery discovered, of accounting shenanigans unearthed and accounting giants unhorsed, of revealed and cleaved sweetheart deals, of an overdose of reality for venture capitalists and investment bankers as the tech stocks went sour, of analysts who knowingly touted bad stocks, of fund mutual managers who got better than they gave, and of excruciating pain for investors. Gone, in one fell swoop, was the glow and warmth of investor confidence. Gone threadbare was the good old cloak of trust and integrity in Wall Street.

It was not just that the market dropped—plummeted is the better word—but that foundations for trust in the people who run companies, in the people who analyze and give presumably knowledgeable and fair recommendations about securities, in the professionals who audit and certify financial statements, crumbled.

Greed has always been with us, as has the hubris that misinforms arrogant individuals of the notion that they're not only above the law, but that they're also beyond punishment. "If I'm smart enough to run a company, I'm smart enough to loot it," they seem to say. The problem is that the few who think this way, and act on it, taint the vast number of honest and diligent corporate leaders. These bad apples are also responsible for stringent laws that affect the honest along with the dishonest.

For the publicly held company that survived, there remained a need to build confidence in its management and to maintain a market for its stock. Never really built on a bed of wisdom, and with a perspective rarely beyond the closing bell of the day's trading, the minions of the market—the brokers, analysts, institutional investors, and so forth—panicked, and like the character in the Stephen Leacock story who jumped on his horse and rode madly off in all directions at once, they led the charge to the four winds.

And as the market slowly began its comeback in early 2004, it did so in new configurations, governed by new regulations designed to insulate investors from chicanery. But alongside the banner of confidence flew the flag of caution.

It should be remembered that for generations, and despite occasional but rare lapses, the probity, integrity and honesty of the financial community was accepted with a greater certitude than in almost any other institution. The motto of Wall Street has long been, "My word is my bond." Well, not any more.

Which is why it isn't your father's investor relations any more.

THE INVESTOR RELATIONS CHALLENGE

If investor relations remains a venue of the financial discipline, it now becomes, as well, the domain of the marketer. Or more accurately to the investor relations professional's acumen must be added the skills—and certainly the viewpoint—of the marketer. A small but significant addition— most investor relations professionals' communications skills are already part of their arsenals. Marketing, in investor relations, is more a frame of reference than an overwhelming configuration of marketing tools. But marketing methods are distinctly part of sound investor relations practice.

Where once the relationship between the company and its investors or potential investors was maintained almost entirely with basic investor relations tools—the analyst meeting, the shareholders meeting, the annual report, the press release—today the concepts of contemporary marketing, driven by the needs and desires of the market and not by the wishes of the company—alter the techniques used. Investor research is more thorough, now, and more is known, and sought to be known, about the prospective investor, so that information can be more relevant to the investor's needs. Today the identified potential investor is pursued with a variety of devices, from Web pages to E-mail.

The traditional investor relations techniques—the analyst meeting and luncheons, the press releases, the annual report—have all changed, as the needs of the investor and the techniques of communication have changed. There are now more intensive attempts to penetrate the consciousness of the investor. Electronics move communication from random and broadcast to targeted. We can know more about our target, and tailor our information to that target, and get the information out there—effectively and cost effectively.

And what has all this to do with the new investor? Simply this.

Every investor is a *customer*. Every investor is a buyer—or seller—of stock, or an intermediary who advises others to buy stock.

If you're squeamish about marketing—OK, even about selling—remember that the role of investor relations is to persuade an investor (read *customer*) that a dollar invested in your company will appreciate faster than a dollar invested in somebody else's company. *Persuasion* means using facts intelligently, and using marketing techniques to project those facts in a way that leads the investor to understand why that dollar invested in your company will appreciate faster than a dollar invested in another company. It does not, under any circumstance, mean distorting or perverting or exaggerating the facts. Good communications means clarity, transparency, and truth. Ask any corporate jailbird.

The elements and foundation of change in the business landscape are now well known. But what has changed most significantly is not just the structure of the markets, nor the regulatory environment generated by the events of the past few years, but the nature and practices of the investor. We live, now, in a world in which more than half of adult Americans own stock. And not all of them have MBAs, nor have many of them even seen Wall Street.

At the same time, it's important to recognize that, as with most things in the dynamics of our world, not everything has changed—and that fact alone dictates a fresh view of the investor, both professional and nonprofessional. And it's the investor, after all, who is the target audience for investor relations.

Ultimately, more than half of corporate capital for American and international business comes from equities. The major portion of the remainder of the capital needed to run even a moderate-sized company must come from either debt or retained earnings (real, not inflated). It must be noted that the profits from which come retained earnings are also the source of dividends. This distribution of earnings becomes an investor relations problem, incidentally, because shareholders must then be made to understand the balance between profits to be distributed and the need for profits to be reinvested. Thus, the case for more aggressive marketing, as an investor relations discipline becomes even more compelling than ever before.

One last word about the stock market.

The stock market is never finite. It's constantly in motion, always changing, always subject to a vast variety of influences. It's easy to think of it in terms of the current market, or yesterday's market or the future market. There are a great many factors that affect the market, and we even know what some of them are, but there are too many factors to know all of them. And for all the science, for all the technology, for all the theories, it's still a wild horse we have to ride, as both investors and as corporations trying to craft the texture of the corporation to match the needs of the market.

It's always the current market, and it will always change. Up or down, it will survive the next disaster, and thrive on the next windfall. But it's always the current market.

Jeffrey Corbin, managing partner of KCSA Worldwide, makes the point in his book, *Investor Relations: The Art of Communicating Value*. He says, "For the publicly traded company, it is important to recognize that the stock market works—that it presents a true valuation of a company." But, he notes, "if a company's communications—in writing or in oral presentations—do not sufficiently explain the current valuation and potential opportunity, the highest possible valuation will not be attained and more damage than good may result."

For the corporation seeking to improve the performance of its own stock, in even the worst of the markets, certain basic facts must be recognized...

- Regardless of the price of a stock at any given moment, or the low to which the Dow Jones average—or any other average—may sink at any moment, there is still a market. It opens every morning and it closes every night. Granted, volume may diminish or expand sharply, but liquidity—or at least the structure for liquidity—still exists.
- The number of firms in the securities industry fluctuates rapidly and wildly. But the industry doesn't cease to exist, even in the worst of times. Despite some severe economic downturns, and profound securities

industry shakeups, the number of firms doing business in the securities industry went from 4470 in 1970 to 9021 by the end of the 1980s. The number of security analysts, those people responsible for analyzing a public corporation's potential for success in the stock market, went from as many as 15,000 in 1971 to 17,000 by the end of the 1980s. In 1997, with the increase in pension fund management and other institutional analysts, there are almost 23,000 analysts registered with the Financial Analysts Federation (now called the Chartered Financial Analysts Federation). By the end of the 1980s, there were 32,000 stock brokers. Today—reflecting the new economic environment—there are more than 74,000 brokers.

During the past four decades we've had several business cycles. We've had recessions and booms, profound inflation and remarkable stability. We've seen new European, Asian, and Middle East economic configurations, and perfidy on Wall Street. We've seen the market attacked by wars and recession.

We've seen, as well, new industries that have revolutionized society, such as technology, biotechnology, and communications. Once glamorous industries, such as steel, have declined, or emerged as mini-industries. Who could have predicted, a few years ago, the ubiquitous cell phone? And through it all, the need for capital has relentlessly grown, and the role of investor relations has grown—its value proven again and again.

What has not changed—what is constant—is the competition for capital. And the way this competition is fought is to add the best skills of marketing to the best practices of investor relations.

COMPETING FOR CAPITAL

What are these marketing skills and techniques, for an investor relations program?

It has long been considered that basic investor relations consisted of just getting the information out to prospective investors and those who advise them. Send out the press release. Hold the analyst meetings. Write the annual report.

This was marketing by default. Communication by hit or miss. It ignored the fact that other corporations were doing the same thing—that there was intensive competition for the same investor's dollar.

Gradually, then, as the competitive role was recognized, the marketing techniques began to take shape, and that's when investor relations became a marketing concept. Under any circumstances, this capital must be competed for against hundreds—thousands—of other corporations for whom growth and infusion of capital is both desirable and imperative.

In order to compete successfully for that capital, any corporation must be prepared to demonstrate—clearly, forcefully, honestly, and skillfully— those factors about itself that indicate that an investment in it is warranted. Today's corporation, recognizing the atmosphere fostered by the chicanery of the past few years, must also go to great lengths to demonstrate not just the facts about itself, but the integrity and accuracy of those facts. Investor skepticism must be overcome before investor confidence can be regained.

Nor can it be assumed that a company's record will speak for itself. True, there are rare occasions when a company's superior performance is discovered, recognized, and rewarded in the marketplace. But for each such company there are dozens of companies whose presidents moan in frustration that the price of their stock in no way reflects the company's performance. Under the best of circumstances nobody is watching. Under the worst of circumstances there is a lethargy and a suspicion that precludes the independent investigation that might turn up a corporate gem and follow it, quarter by quarter, through superior performance.

It might be assumed that the better product, and the better company, will of itself be discovered and embraced by an eager investment community. But that would be naïve. There are too many dynamic forces at work in the capital markets to presume that even finding a cure for the common cold will project a company's stock market success.

A case in point is Checkpoint Software, a leading producer of firewall software to protect the integrity and security of internet traffic. Checkpoint, a NASDAQ company based in Israel and the United States, had some 40% of the firewall market. It's stock had risen phenomenally. But its success put it under constant assault. Microsoft, a Checkpoint partner, threatened to enter the market with its own product in order to force a better financial arrangement with Checkpoint. The stock plummeted. At a later point, when the stock had recovered to a healthy price/earnings ratio it was assaulted by short sellers and day traders. And so on. It took a healthy investor relations program to keep the Checkpoint stock on an even keel.

A study, using membership in the National Investor Relations Institute as a valid assumption of investor relations activity, discovered that companies with NIRI members on staff have more analysts following their stock than do companies without NIRI members (and therefore, it may be assumed, are without formal investor relations programs). It was also discovered that the greater the number of analysts following a company, the higher its price/earnings ratio. According to a report of the study in the NIRI publication, *Investor Relations Update,* an attempt was made to determine, through regression analysis, whether other factors—profit margins, better returns on assets, superior growth, etc. might account for the results of the study. This analysis offered no other explanation than the investor relations program.

One of the most compelling reasons for an intensive investor relations program during a down market—as well as during an up market—lies in the basic nature of security analysis itself. The greatest part of analysis is based upon intangible and immeasurable factors, such as management and the company's ability to plan and meet its objectives. The more precisely and clearly the elements that define these intangibles are projected, the more readily the company's ability to appreciate the invested dollar will be understood. The more readily this ability is understood, the more likely the acceptance—and investment—by a financial community that discounts for the unknown—the risk.

WHAT THE INVESTOR WANTS TO KNOW

Essentially, the successful investor relations program seeks to demonstrate three basic things to persuade the investor of the success and potential of your company. These are factors that attempt to demonstrate to the investor and the security analyst a company's ability to succeed in the future—to increase the value of its equity and to use its capital effectively. These factors, discussed in greater detail in Chapter 6, depend upon an extraordinarily complex structure of characteristics, but still they all evolve to three basic points...

- Earnings and other measures of financial soundness
- Management
- Plans

Earnings, cash flow, and sound balance sheet and financial structure are, after all, what a corporation is all about. They represent the return on the investment. They signify the company's ability to succeed as a corporation. They demonstrate the soundness of a company, and if a track record of financial stability and growth is present, they may even attest to the company's ability to sustain that soundness and growth.

But at best, earnings, and even cash flow at any given moment, constitute only a small portion of the measure of a company's viability, and they demonstrate not the near future but the immediate past. It's the degree to which the pattern of financial performance demonstrates the ability of the company to continue to earn that must be projected. It's the degree to which financial performance and other factors contribute value to the company and its securities. In today's dynamic world, the random events that can adversely or favorably affect a company proliferate.

It should be remembered, too, that not only do circumstances and conditions change at a rapid rate, but they, and the results of the change, are accessible in real time to the investor and analyst.

Consider a picture of Times Square at high noon, freezing the motion of people and vehicles and even weather at that moment. A picture of the same view taken at 12:01 would be quite different. People and vehicles would be in different positions, and perhaps even the weather will have changed. Compare that view of Times Square, still photo by still photo, with a motion picture of the same view. You now begin to get a sense of the dynamic of a company's condition in an economic environment that that changes constantly.

What makes this even more interesting, in considering the view of a company by its investing public, is that the changing conditions, the changing view, the dynamic of the economy and the company—all are instantly visible to the investing community via the internet.

Thus, analysis has changed. And thus, the nature of investor relations has changed, if only because the investor and the analyst understand this dynamic, and demand that information be supplied, as often as possible, in real time.

But if earnings and cash flow and balance sheet and overall financial performance were the sole measure of a company's potential as an investment vehicle, there would be no auction market. It would all be done by computer. What's more to the point is not just the earnings record of a company, nor even the consistency of its positive cash flow and earnings growth.

The second factor is *management*. A corporation may, by definition, have a perpetual life, but its ability to operate successfully is a function of its management during the tenure of the individual managers. This is as true of a $2 million company as it is of Microsoft, for all its vast size and greatness. If, during the next few years, Bill Gates, the chairman of Microsoft, makes a decision about the computer industry that differs from others in his industry, it will alter the entire structure of Microsoft—and perhaps the entire computer industry—for many generations to come.

The boom years of the late 1990s produced an odd management phenomenon called the *cult of personality*. In fact, it may well have contributed to the corporate excess of the period. This was a situation in which CEOs of major companies, given overwhelming credit for management success, became stars—super CEOs. Jack Welch, of GE. Bill Gates of Microsoft. Warren Buffett of Berkshire Insurance. And so forth. They became legends in both corporate and public annals. Executive compensation rose to proportions that, in too many cases, seemed outlandish, and began to cause alarm by shareholders. While in some cases, adulation and significant compensation were warranted, in too many other cases bonuses and compensation packages were granted in spite of poor performance, rather than because of great performance.

At the same time, this cult of personality became, for some, very heady stuff, and led to the excesses that bred the disasters uncovered in the first years of the 21st century. This is the behavior that led to the revolutionary regulation that now characterizes the corporate world. It bred, as well, a distrust of corporate management at a time when that trust was needed to buoy the investment world. Not only does management now have to project its skill, it has to defend its integrity. Again, the sins of the few are visited upon the vast number of honest executives.

And what, then, must now be projected about management? Not just the skill, intelligence, vigor, and clear-sightedness of its officers, but its ability to see the company, the industry, and the economy clearly. It's the ability of the management team to deal with the day-by-day problems of the company, and its ability to develop and implement realistic long-range plans. It's the ability to fathom all aspects of management—operations, administration, production, marketing, distribution, finance. It's the ability to deal with contingencies in changing situations. Is the management that brought the company from $10 million to $100 million in volume capable of dealing with the same company when its volume reaches $10 billion, and therefore with an entirely new set of problems and opportunities?

Third is *plans*. What is the company going to do tomorrow or five years from now? What are its long range strategic programs? Where is it going? What are its objectives—long, medium, and short range? How does it intend to finance its plans? Are its plans realistic in terms of the industry, the market, the economy, management's abilities, and the company's financial condition? In these dynamic times, circumstances quickly turn positive to negative, as new technology obsolesces old technology. How nimble is management in its ability to change course as market or economic conditions change?

The word *vision* is now popular, and like many popular words, it has become a fad word. Too bad, because vision is a word of substance in management, and in judging management. In fact, *vision,* in management, may be said to be a projection of the outer reaches of possibility. It is not only the vision of a corporate leader that must be projected and judged, it's the assessment of his or her ability to make that vision a reality. When Carly Fiorina of H-P envisioned the value of merging with Compaq, it seemed far-fetched. But she accomplished it, and turned a far-fetched vision into a successful company. She saw the need, in the future, to change the configuration of H-P, and the way to do it. She fought off the naysayers, who were cursed with the lack of her vision. She made it happen.

It is this kind of vision that distinguishes a manager and distinguishes the manager's company. It is this kind of management skill that must be projected to the investment community, if it is to trust the company to use its invested capital well.

When all of these factors about a corporation are projected and understood by the financial community, and when they are projected believably and consistently, then that company can expect to compete successfully in the capital markets. In fact, to the degree that predictability is possible, there is a premium that accrues to it.

OBJECTIVES

No strategic investor relations plan—nor any marketing plan—can be effective without a clear view of objectives. After all, if you don't know where you're going, how do you know how to get there? If you don't have a clearly defined sense of why you're putting yourself through all these machinations, then why are you doing it?

Objectives, like visions, must be concrete and realistic if they are to have any value at all. Not wishes, but goals to be achieved to make a vision a reality. Well-formulated objectives make a vision a working tool for a firm's growth and success. It's crucial, then, that the objectives be precisely defined, in terms of the realistic ability of a practice to meet those objectives. They are, in fact, business decisions.

In an investor relations program, well-formulated objectives are a guide for choosing your target audiences, defining your company in terms of your value to the target group of investors, and defining and managing the investor relations and marketing tools.

The objectives for an investor relations program begin, naturally, with the capital needs of the company. But there are other very specific factors that differ from company to company, from industry to industry. In defining investor relations objectives, three specific elements are paramount...

- *Your company.* Where are you now and where do you want to be? What are your plans for growth and expansion? What is your time frame? What are the opportunities for your company's products and services? Is market expansion viable and realistic? Can you manage growth? In what kind of increments do you plan your growth? What are your plans for research and development to help you compete in a changing economic environment? What are your contingency plans if there is a downturn in the economy? How do you plan to market your products or services? And ultimately, how much money do you need for your future, and how do you plan to use it?
- *The economic environment.* The economy itself is an external factor over which you have no control. It should, however, be a significant element in determining your objectives. Because business invariably runs in cycles, and the economic environment changes, your objectives are a function of the ability to understand and relate to these changes. A case in point is the rapid growth of the computer industry as new technology became an integral part of doing business, and which then dropped off as a saturation point was reached, along with a lull in new technology. It began to change again as we entered a new era of communication that has been tantamount to an industrial revolution that affected even low tech companies.
- *The capital markets.* Obviously, the ability to raise capital at any given time is a function of the capital markets. While there are many sources of capital, the flexibility of those sources changes dramatically in response to innumerable stimuli. There are trends and cycles, and while there are always exceptions, as a general rule it's not a good idea to try to raise capital for a company with a speculative idea in a tight market.

Codifying these objectives helps to develop an investor relations program that's relevant to your needs as a company, and relevant to your company in pursuing capital to meet those needs.

MEASURING INVESTOR RELATIONS PERFORMANCE

Ultimately, the success of an investor relations program is measured by the degree to which it meets its defined objectives. This is not a simple answer. While, in the long run, the major objective is to attain capital raising goals, and to increase the value of a company's securities, the time frame for accomplishing this may be beyond the control of any company. A speculative company—one with a new management or new product or new market—will take longer to be recognized by the capital markets than a company with technology for solving a major medical problem. One company with a successful investor relations program may achieve a high volume and high price/earnings ratio in a very short time. Another, with a successful investor relations program, may take longer to be recognized by the markets. Some programs need more time, others less time, to meet defined objectives.

How, then, is success in an investor relations program measured?

It is measured in a feedback of knowledge and understanding about a company and its management by those segments of the financial community that are most important to that corporation.

It is reflected in the relative ease with which a corporation can deal with the capital markets, ranging from banks to the equities market.

It is reflected in a realistic price/earnings or price/cash flow ratio, in relation to the overall average price/earnings or P/CF ratio of the stock market in any given time and, more significantly, a corporation's own industry.

It is reflected in increased liquidity—the comparative ease with which sellers find buyers and buyers find sellers, even in a sparse market, and in increased trading activity.

It is measured in the increased valuation of a company's securities in the market.

It is reflected in increased and enthusiastic sponsorship and more market makers and supporters, and, if appropriate, in geographic distribution of the issue.

It builds trust in management—an important factor in view of the events leading to the new regulatory environment. (A clue to the revival of investor trust comes clear amid all the bewailing of the minions of the Street—and that clue is the word *fundamentals.*)

Investor relations is not an action—it's a process. It takes time, and effort, and patience. It informs, it persuades, it educates. In other words, it *markets.*

And so where once investor relations was simply a useful tool applied by some very bright company managers and their equally capable investor relations agents, it's now an integral part of the investment process itself—a primary pipeline of information that's at the very heart of the investment process.

MARKETING IN A NUTSHELL

The best practices of marketing, whether for a product, a service, or a stock, consist of four basic elements...

- Know your market
- Know your product
- Know your marketing tools
- Manage your tools

These elements translate, for investor relations, thus...

Know your market. Your market, in this case, is the investor. This includes the professional investors—institutions, money managers, mutual funds—and private investors. In investor relations, it includes, as well, those who function as intermediaries—the analysts, the brokers, and the institutional sales force—who recommend and who sell the stock. But as might be expected, each category of investors has its own requirements for investing, its own needs for information, and its own techniques in processing that information.

To know your market, then, means more than having lists of institutions and money managers. It means understanding the nuances of each group—its special purposes, its needs, its accessibility and significantly, the means to reach each group. It means understanding, as well, the relationship between what your company has to offer to each of these investing groups, and how well their needs are met by your company and its stock.

Knowing your market means understanding that the dynamics of the stock market change at a rapid pace, and that what was true yesterday may not be true today or tomorrow. The circumstances affecting a financial market are in constant flux, affected by myriad events, such as the nature of the market itself, the economy, weather, war, geography, and dozens of other factors.

Until not too long ago, corporate business and financial information was punctuated by defined time frames. Annually and quarterly. Frequently, by the time the information about a company became available, the information had changed. Today, through technology, data is available dynamically—as it changes, the changes are known instantly. The investors know this. Corporate management should know it too.

Essentially, there are three general categories of investors that are the sources of capital, and that comprise your target audiences...

- The professional investor—the institutional investor and the money manager
- The investment advisor—the analyst, broker and other advisors who recommend stock and influence decisions
- The individual investor—the retail stock buyer and the 401(k) investor

Each group has its specific needs, and each is accessible in different ways, and with different techniques. Each is able to transform information into action to its own purposes.

Know your company. Yes, you know your company. But the point is to know your company in terms of the potential audience—the market—for your stock is to see it in terms of the market's needs or interests.

There are four basic elements that define a company's value in the capital markets and that influence buying decisions...

- *Financial data*—the numbers, the performance, the stock values in the market. This is now commonly called the *metrics*—a fad word to describe traditional data.
- *The industry*—the company's position in the industry, the strength of the industry itself, the company's markets, the company's plans for the future
- *The economy*—the broader context against which investment decisions are made
- *Management*—its strength and depth, its capabilities, its credibility, its ability to make plans a reality and to cope with changing environments (e.g. AOL's ability to cope with a saturated computer market and a decline in advertising revenues)

We will explore these elements in Chapter 6, but in terms of knowing your company, they give us a specific view that relates what you are to what the market for your securities needs. These four points give you a clue of how to present your company to your market in ways that specifically address their needs.

It really is a form of self-examination. Are your financial results—revenues, earnings per share, cash flow, balance sheet items, stock float, and so forth—consistent with the needs of your target audience (read *potential investors*)? We have always understood that there are different investors for small cap companies and for large international companies, but by matching who you are with the groups of potential investors that are partial to companies with your financial configuration allows you to focus your message to those groups.

Most companies are part of a specific industry, and are judged by specialists in those industries. One need only look at the rise and fall and rise again of high tech companies to understand that there is a tide in industry analysis that tends to bring the same judgment to good companies in a declining industry as to bad companies. This is a problem that can only be addressed, though, by recognizing, first, that this kind of judgment exists, and second, that there are ways it can be overcome. In any marketing context, distinguishing one company from its competitors is a substantial aspect of marketing.

Obviously, the economic context makes a difference. When the economy is booming, faith in the rise of the market, and in the cornucopia of return on investment, is high. Buying decisions, whether made by institutional or individual investors, tend to be made more on hope—on *riding the wave*—than on analysis of principles. When the economy is static, declining, or uncertain, faith is tempered by anxiety. The stock market, remember, is a function of future—of a promise of good things to come. When the economic factors that seem to be beyond any individual's control offer less hope, then stock purchases are made more cautiously, if not more rationally. Economic conditions pose different relationships between your company's message and the target audiences.

Of the four elements, the most important to project is management. To a large degree, the first three factors are readily discernable. The facts about a company's performance are readily available to everyone, as they should be, although every investor interprets the data differently. The state of the economy is rarely beyond anybody's ken. The wild card—and the factor that must be projected most carefully—is management. At the same time, the techniques for using all four factors to shape the perception of the company as a viable investment vehicle must be meticulously defined and presented to the investing public and those who advise them.

Know your marketing tools. The tools—the mechanics—of projecting the elements of your company are all standard. They are as available to you and every other company seeking to sell its equities. And while we will discuss these tools in greater detail further on, it is important to realize that, like carpenter's tools in the hands of a master cabinet maker, they are merely tools. The cabinet maker makes masterpieces with the skill and artistry with which those tools are used, and it is the skill and artistry that makes the masterpiece—not the tools. This is the secret of all marketing. This is the secret of successful investor relations.

Manage your tools. Assuming a grasp of the skills and techniques of investor relations practice, the successful investor relations program—the one that helps you compete best for the investment dollar—is a function of strategy and planning. It is a function, as well, of understanding all of these four elements, and using them strategically and artfully.

In the final analysis, an effective investor relations program is an effective marketing program.

CHAPTER 3

Regulation

Rules of Disclosure—
The SEC and Sarbanes-Oxley

At the core of all investor relations practice is the concept of disclosure. Disclosure is, as well, at the core of the marketing thrust of investor relations. In investor relations, disclosure means transparency—the ability of all investors, equally, to know what needs to be known about a corporation in order to make investment decisions on a par with all other investors.

This is the philosophy, and it's a good one, despite any tendency by a corporation's management to hide unpleasant facts, or to give advantage to one group of investors over another. It's a good philosophy because, ultimately, the better informed the investing public is, the greater the likelihood for trust in the company's integrity, and, therefore, the greater support for its stock. Certainly, integrity is very much the issue. The scandals at the turn of the 21st century caused a dim public eye to be cast on the many honest and well-managed firms, at the behest of the scandalous behavior of a few rogue corporate leaders.

Human nature being what it is, and for reasons arising historically from the failure of corporate America's ability to see the virtues of corporate transparency in an era of cavalier chicanery in the 1920s and 1930s, the United States Congress, in the Securities Exchange Act of 1934, created the U.S. Securities and Exchange Commission (SEC), and promulgated Rules of Disclosure, to be administered by the SEC. The purpose of disclosure regulations is to assure the public equal and timely access to all information that might affect the price and market value of a security. The regulations attempt to preclude trading on inside information—both good and bad news—that might cause disadvantage to those not privy to that information at the same time as every other investor. The U.S. SEC and, in some cases, state authorities, regulate those companies whose securities are traded on exchanges or NASDAQ.

Subsequently, as economic circumstances changed, and as new aspects of regulation required it, the rules may have been tweaked by defining regulations, but the underlying principle has remained the same.

As a result of the flaunting and flagrant disregard of securities laws and acts of fraud in the first years of the 21st century, new legislation— The Sarbanes-Oxley Act of 2002 and Regulation FD—*Regulation Fair Disclosure*—was created. These new laws and regulations elevate and strengthen not only the Rules of Disclosure, but alter, as well, the practices of accounting and accounting firms, of securities firms and analysts, and the governance of corporations. If the Securities Exchange Act of 1934 was volcanic in its time, then the Sarbanes-Oxley Act is revolutionary in this generation.

Prior to the securities acts of 1933 and 1934, corporate disclosure was minimal. In 1926 all corporations whose stocks were listed on the New York Stock Exchange published balance sheets showing current assets and current liabilities. In these statements only 71% showed depreciation, 45% showed the cost of goods sold, and 55% showed sales. Today, it would be unthinkable for any published report of a public corporation not to include this and a great deal of other pertinent information. And even so, it's only within the past decade that corporate annual reports routinely break down performance by lines of business, whether by division or product line or other business segmentation. Until the SEC made it mandatory to do so, there were still relatively few companies that included in their annual reports information that covers the range of material demanded by law in the Corporate Annual Report Form 10-K.

For generations, the concept of disclosure was inimical to the early giants of industry, who felt that because they founded their companies, what they did was their own business, and even investors had no say in how a company should run. "If you don't like the way the stock is behaving," they said, "then sell it—but don't tell us how to run the company." The SEC's enforcement personnel had hard corporate shells to penetrate, and it took many years for many companies to stop fighting the regulations. And even so, many companies sought, and found, chinks in the enforcement process. Unfortunately for many of them, the chinks became loopholes, the loopholes led to license, and the license led to indictment. And for the rest—

even the overwhelming majority of honest corporate managers—came Regulation FD and The Sarbanes-Oxley Act of 2002.

THE SEC

All publicly traded securities are regulated by the United States Securities and Exchange Commission, a federal regulatory body established by Congress under the Securities Exchange Act of 1934. Its chair and commission members are appointed by the president of the United States. It has a very large and enthusiastic staff, with offices in major cities throughout the United States, as well as in Washington, D.C. Its major assignment is to regulate and monitor the offer to sell and trade securities for virtually all public companies, stock exchanges, and securities dealers in the country. A major objective is to assure that all investors have equal and timely access to all information material to the decisions to buy or sell a stock, by virtue of rather stringent rules of disclosure, and that the material is accurate. It does its job well and takes it seriously.

As is the case with any governmental agency, it generally takes on the character of the administration it serves, as well as the commission's chairperson. But regardless of the administration, or its chair, or in its emphasis on any particular aspect of securities regulation, it never strays from its basic purpose.

In response to the public reaction to the misdeeds of a number of corporations and accounting firms, and with the strictures of the Sarbanes-Oxley Act and other legislation, enforcement of the law is swift and stringent. The SEC, at this writing, is headed by William H. Donaldson, a long-time leading figure on Wall Street and former chairman of the New York Stock Exchange. Under his aegis, the SEC is swiftly and firmly bringing securities regulation into a new era, and bringing new vigor into enforcement. In addition to securities regulation, the SEC now deals as well with the management and structure of the New York Stock Exchange, the National Association of Securities Dealers and NASDAQ, with the accounting and legal professions, with corporate governance, with financial services organizations, and even with law firms in SEC practice—with myriad other issues within its purview that had been long ignored, or which have been newly addressed by legislation. Mr. Donaldson has also been given wider authority by the Sarbanes-Oxley Act, and additional funds (an increase of 66% for 2003) to support the agency's regulatory actions.

At the same time, following a compensation scandal involving the chairman of the New York Stock Exchange—now the former chairman—the NYSE is being reorganized, for both efficiency and relevancy to the needs of its members, its listed companies, and their shareholders.

Among SEC initiatives are efforts to give shareholders in a corporation more say in nominating board members and in having greater voice in corporate initiatives and management; in regulating mutual funds, and particularly the lightly regulated hedge funds; in increasing disclosure rules under existing and new laws; in instituting and reporting corporate codes of ethics; in monitoring the actions of security analysts; in monitoring the structure of audit committees under the new regulations of Sarbanes-Oxley, and much more. Moreover, the SEC now publishes online its comments on many companies' filings.

It should be noted that Sarbanes-Oxley not only grants new powers to the SEC, and that the Congress and the administration have allocated larger amounts of funding (increasing the funding for 2003 by 66%), but that under Mr. Donaldson, the SEC is proving to be more active and innovative than it's been at any time in recent history. Its initiatives go much beyond enforcement to build a new body of regulation to enable not only the letter of the law, but its spirit as well. However, in spite of the increased funding, the SEC found difficulty in recruiting sufficient lawyers and accountants to handle the increased regulatory load. This is due to competition from the private sector and the newly formed Public Company Accounting Oversight Board (PCAOB).

This newly charged SEC poses a major challenge to corporate investor relations officers, which, in the words of Louis M. Thomson, Jr., president and CEO of the National Investor Relations Institute (NIRI), is to move "from opaque disclosure that complies with the rules to investor relations communications that are compliant but transparent—communications that are clear, concise, and comprehensible."

Each state also has its body of securities laws and regulations, most of which are enforced by the state attorney general. These laws are known as *blue sky laws*, since they were originally designed—many of them prior to the establishment of the SEC—to prevent unscrupulous securities dealers from promising and selling investors everything but the blue sky.

All companies selling securities to the public must conform to the laws and regulations of both the SEC and every state in which those securities are sold.

All exchanges have rules and regulations governing disclosure practices of companies whose stock is listed—traded—on those exchanges. Naturally, these regulations are often developed to parallel, comply with, or function to complement SEC and state regulation. The exchanges, including NASDAQ however, frequently define or expand the regulations for listed companies.

The vast body of regulations covers every aspect of security practices, particularly those that affect the value of that company's stock in the public market. The regulatory concern here is principally with the legal aspects of the dissemination of that information—the Rules of Disclosure.

THE SARBANES-OXLEY ACT OF 2002

Alarmed by what it perceived to be an epidemic of corporate and accounting fraud, Congress passed the Sarbanes-Oxley Act of 2002. It revolutionized the nature of the public corporation in the United States—making what is perhaps the most significant body of new securities law in 70 years.

More than just new regulations addressing the relations between corporations and their shareholders, it changes decades—generations—of corporate practices and corporate governance, of accounting practices, of traditions and responsibilities in the legal profession, and in financial firm practices.

The new Sarbanes-Oxley Act . . .

- Mandates new rules regarding the composition and duties of boards of directors, putting greater responsibilities on the boards' audit committees. No longer can boards be comprised of barely qualified relatives and friends, but must include a majority of independent outsiders. The audit committee, now at the heart of corporate financial certification, can no longer be comprised of insiders with little or no financial expertise, but must now include outsiders with proven financial statement expertise. Retaining and monitoring the corporation's auditors, auditor consulting contracts, and 401(k) plans are no longer the province of management, but are now the purview of the audit committee. This is a radical reversal of corporate practice, and takes from the hands of management a great deal of traditional responsibility for financial controls and puts more responsibility on the Board of Directors. Under these rules, the failure of directors and officers to comply with the new requirements would constitute a breach of duty of care, and the SEC might declare an individual unfit to be a public officer or director, with substantial personal penalties.

- Creates a new structure to oversee the accounting profession for publicly traded companies. The new Public Company Accounting Oversight Board (PCAOB) is required to review annually all CPA firms that serve publicly traded companies. All public accounting firms must be registered by the PCAOB in order to be eligible to audit public companies. For decades, the accounting profession has relied on self-regulation, and has fought off congressional and other governmental attempts at regulation from outside the profession. However, following a rash of cases in which accounting firms were found to have severely violated accounting rules, and certainly following the demise of Arthur Andersen, one of the world's largest accounting firms, for its role in the Enron scandal, the government felt it could no longer rely upon the accounting profession to regulate itself. Thus, PCAOB.

- Makes it a crime to destroy or conceal documents in order to impede a federal investigation. Arthur Andersen's shredding material documents was integral to the fraud case against Enron and the accounting firm.

- Limits consulting practice as part of the accounting and audit practice. What had begun some decades ago as an auditor's service to clients, assisting in non-accounting related business consulting and in establishing and managing a client's financial systems and controls, ultimately began to grow beyond the boundaries of true independence. What actually happened in most cases was that the consulting practice of a client-CPA relationship became so lucrative that some accounting firms couldn't resist client entreaties to fudge an audit to keep the consulting business. This is one of the significant practices that led to a rash of corporate scandals, and that precipitated the Sarbanes-Oxley Act.

- Requires CEOs and CFOs to certify the accuracy of financial reports. Following the scandals, it became clear that either the CEOs and CFOs were completely ignorant of the financial aspects of their companies, or that they were using ignorance to excuse themselves from responsibility for their companies' fraud. They can no longer say, in effect, "I didn't know the gun was loaded."

- Requires that managers annually report on the effectiveness of internal control over financial reporting, and that auditors regularly scrutinize and evaluate these controls. This regulation implementing

Section 404 of the Sarbanes-Oxley Act puts a spotlight on internal controls, and demands strict establishment and management of these controls. A discussion of the internal controls must be included in annual reports. While companies have used internal financial controls to protect the company against fraud and other unethical behavior, management must now acknowledge that responsibility, and have the efficacy of these controls assessed and attested to by the company's auditors.

- Forces CEOs to give up gains from stock options and bonuses granted on the basis of false reporting. It also makes it easier to criminally prosecute corporate executives who destroy evidence (as was done in the Enron and other cases) or to defraud investors. Lying to the SEC and otherwise committing fraudulent acts now means extensive fines and lengthened prison terms imposed by the Justice Department and States Attorneys general. The SEC has civil authority to levy fines and restrain the perpetrator from further participation in the securities markets, and serving as an officer or director of a public company.

- Requires executives to disclose their stock sales within two days, which is a weapon against insider trading.

- Requires shareholder approval of option plans, as part of the effort to increase shareholder democracy.

- Creates a raft of new filing regulations, including limitations on the use of non-GAAP *(Generally Accepted Accounting Principles)* financial measures. Regulation G adds to the general disclosure principles of the anti-fraud provisions of the 1934 Securities Exchange Act. It provides that if a registrant furnishes to the SEC or publicly discloses a non-GAAP financial measure it must first make a presentation of the most directly comparable financial measure calculated in accordance with GAAP, and then provide a reconciliation that's quantitative for both historical and prospective measures of the differences between the non-GAAP financial measure and the most directly comparable GAAP measure. NIRI's Louis Thompson notes that "Congress and the SEC wanted to take the mystery out of earnings, and help investors understand a company's true results. I also believe," he added, "that there's a recognition at both the SEC and FASB (Financial Accounting Standards Board) that GAAP itself is not an end all." Professor Baruch Lev, of the Stern School of Business at New York University, is quoted in the NIRI publication *Standards of Practice For Investor Relations,* as pointing out that more than half of the average S&P 500 company's market value is due to intangible assets. Regulation G also says that releases must be posted on the company's web site, which, Thompson points out, alters the way news is to be disseminated.

- Allows workers to diversify 401(k) plans away from company stock holdings after being at the firm for 3 years.
- Requires the SEC to formulate rules preventing analysts' conflict of interest.
- Mandates corporate codes of ethics.

The radical nature and stringency of Sarbanes-Oxley controls were, naturally, not universally greeted with joy by every segment of management. A question arose about the effect of the Act on the role of the chief financial officer, whose duties under the Act were most affected. The Act, for example, requires that authority to hire external auditors now goes to the board's audit committee—and takes it away from the CFO. Yet, a poll by *CFO* magazine of more than 300 senior finance executives finds them split on whether the governance reforms enacted by the Act are worth the considerable effort of implementing them. They are also divided about whether CFOs should work merely to satisfy the letter of the law or go further and embrace its spirit.

The poll showed, however, that despite the shift of responsibility mandated by the Sarbanes-Oxley, fully 70 percent of finance executives believe the CFO's standing ultimately will be enhanced. Talks by the magazine's editors with finance executives, academics, activists, and experts in the governance field strongly suggest that the emergence of these more influential finance chiefs will depend in large measure on their response to a new corporate world in which power is more diffuse and penalties are substantially increased.

In the months following the enactment of Sarbanes-Oxley, the cost of compliance increased substantially for the 14,000 companies that trade publicly. One estimate is that the annual cost of being public nearly doubled, from $1.3 million to almost $2.5 million. Several companies are said to have withdrawn initial public offerings because of the compliance costs. And yet, the beginning of 2004 showed an increase in new offerings, which simply means that the need for capital trumps the cost of capital and the efforts to get it. FedEx reported that implementation of Section 404 alone cost approximately $20 million.

At the same time, as Sarbanes-Oxley is integrated into the corporate practice, it's proving its ability to define best corporate practice. And by demonstrating compliance, it informs the investor of corporate integrity.

An interesting sidebar to Sarbanes-Oxley is that an increasing number of non-public companies, not required to abide by Sarbanes-Oxley regulations, are nevertheless doing so. They say that the regulations serve as models of good management. Furthermore, should they ultimately go public, their experience in complying with the law should help them in the marketplace. This is also true with foreign-based companies listed on the NYSE and NASDAQ as ADRs.

Most significantly, the SEC and the U.S. Department of Justice have already begun to indict corporate officers who have violated statutes of Sarbanes-Oxley. Sarbanes-Oxley is not an empty drum.

REGULATION FD

In 2000, beset by a rash of companies selectively disclosing material non-public information to investors and analysts, and by growing seepage in the foundations of disclosure regulations, the SEC promulgated Regulation FD—*Regulation Fair Disclosure.*

What FD did was to insure that everybody had equal access to the same information at the same time and to limit insider trading, particularly in areas of limited disclosure of inside information. FD was designed as one more step in leveling the playing field for the non-insider investor. And like all such regulatory strictures, it altered the nature of investor relations.

Public disclosure means dissemination of information through the media, and includes press releases, and an 8-K and other filings. The test of appropriate media is that it must be designed to effect broad non-exclusionary distribution of the information to the public.

If material non-public information is inadvertently disclosed to an individual or narrow group of individuals in this category, the company must immediately publicly disclose the information to the public. If the disclosure is unintentional, the information must be disclosed to the public within 24 hours, or before the start of the next trading day.

FD specifically designates four categories of people to whom selective disclosure many not be made—broker-dealers and their staff (primarily, analysts); investment advisors and certain institutional managers; investment companies, such as hedge funds; and shareholders at a time when it might be assumed that they might act on the information.

Exempted from FD are *temporary insiders* (such as lawyers, investment bankers, or accountants) who, by virtue of their positions, owe the company trust or confidence; the media, securities rating agencies, and ordinary course business communications with customers and suppliers. The regulation doesn't apply to foreign issuers.

Parenthetically, NIRI's Lou Thompson notes, "If an analyst or investor were to threaten a company with a loss of coverage or reducing their investment if it didn't give them material, nonpublic information, he or she could be liable for violating the rule."

Regulation FD is also designed to address the threat to the integrity of the market from corporate management's potential ability to treat material information as a commodity to be used to gain favor with specific analysts or investors. It's a powerful mandate for corporations to bring transparency to their financial and business operations, so that every investor is making investment decisions with the same information. How each investor uses that information is, of course, another matter. But as long as it's done within the boundaries of law, it's not the concern of regulatory agencies.

Significantly, surveys show that companies with a more open disclosure policy experience lower stock price volatility, a tighter range of earnings estimates, and a lower cost of capital. Sarbanes-Oxley suggests that companies create a disclosure committee to oversee the internal financial control process.

While Regulation FD offers new and needed protection, NIRI points out to its members that the law makes more urgent the need for companies to establish written disclosure policies where they don't now exist.

It should be noted here that both Sarbanes-Oxley and Regulation FD place a good measure of responsibility in the hands of investor relations officers. They are the specialists and experts in the new law, fully understand the law's ramifications, and are expert in communications to investors and the financial community. At the same time, by demonstrating to the investing and financial communities the integrity fostered by adherence and compliance with the law, they serve to enhance trust in the companies they serve.

In the early days of investor relations, when securities law was more lax, and the relations between corporations and investors were not fully appreciated, investor relations practice was ancillary to the corporate process.

This is no longer the case. For the public company today, investor relations is an integral part of management. In fact, a growing number of corporations now invite investor relations officers to participate in management and board meetings. This practice can only redound to enhanced relations between the corporation and the investing public, and greater success for the corporation in the marketplace.

COMPLIANCE WITH SECURITIES LAW

It would be a simpler world if the rules for disclosure were more clear cut. But this is a complex world, in which so many seemingly simple solutions to apparently simple problems are thwarted by conditions and circumstances and conflicting opinions and levels of regulations and regulatory requirements that conflict with the best interests of the company, that corporate, legal and financial judgment is invariably crucial to compliance.

A case in point is the Schering-Plough action, in which the SEC cited the company's former CEO, Richard Kogan, for violation of Regulation FD.

During meetings with analysts and fund managers of several of Schering's largest investors on September 9, 2003, Mr. Kogan imparted information that differed from the company's earlier statements. This information was not disseminated to the general investing public. In three following days, armed with this information, two of the attending group, Fidelity and Putnam, each sold more than 10 million shares, which caused market activity that resulted in a 17% decline in the stock's price. No media release was issued. On October 3, 2003, a previously scheduled meeting with some 25 analysts and investors was held, at which participants were informed that Schering's 2003 earnings would be "terrible". That evening, a press release was finally issued, but as NIRI's Lou Thompson pointed out, it was too late. The damage had been done.

For violating Regulation FD, Schering paid a million dollar fine, and Kogan paid a $50,000 fine.

Should one question the reason for strong enforcement of securities law, one need only look at the case of Siebel Systems, which came on the heels of the Schering-Plough action. What's more startling is that Siebel had already paid a $250,000 civil penalty in November 2002, for violation of FD, based upon remarks made at an investor conference.

Despite this history of FD violations, company executives, in April 2004, selectively disclosed information that unfairly affected the movement of the stock, according to a report in the *Wall Street Journal*. Early in April, the company had indicated that it wouldn't meet earlier forecasts of earnings. However, on April 30, management met privately with two fund managers and told them that sales activity had improved, and that the company had deals in the pipeline. Immediately following the meeting, two of the fund managers who had attended but didn't own Siebel stock then purchased 114,200 shares while the market was still open. A third manager, informed of the meeting, covered a short position of 108,00 shares.

On the evening of April 30, Siebel managers made a speech at a dinner hosted by Morgan Stanley. The next morning, Morgan Stanley sent e-mails to hundreds of individuals, describing the "positive data points" from the dinner. Two fund managers who attended the dinner bought Siebel shares the next morning. "That day," the *Wall Street Journal* reported, "Siebel shares jumped 8% to $9.34, with trading volume nearly double the average daily volume for the previous 12 months, the SEC said."

While there may be no question that imparting material information to a few without disseminating it to the larger public was a clear violation of Regulation FD, other questions arose. Did the size of the group to whom the original material was disclosed, by both Schering-Plough and Siebel, constitute a one-on-one meeting? And if so, does that mean that one-on-one meetings, long traditional in investor relations practice, are no longer possible?

Not necessarily, as long as the rules of immediate disclosure are followed. A caution, though. One-on-one meetings offer the danger of inadvertent disclosure. At the same time the practice gives rise to the question of whether the potential risk is worth any potential advantage. Remember, too, that one of the purposes of FD is to avoid using advanced information to curry favor with a particular group of analysts, money managers, or investors. Is the perceived advantage of a one-on-one meeting worth the need to follow such discussions with the full battery of disclosure activities? Generally, the value of such meetings, beyond the attempt to curry favor with one or more analysts or investors, is to offer the opportunity to meet with, and assess, management—a worthwhile effort. But attention must be paid to avoid inadvertent disclosure of material information.

NIRI's Lou Thompson points out an interesting aspect of the Siebel case by noting that the SEC cited the company's former investors relations officer for failure to maintain proper disclosure controls to prevent violation of Regulation FD. According to the SEC's complaint Siebel appointed

Mark Hanson as head of the company's IR department and "directed Hanson to ensure that the company did 'everything possible' to comply with Regulation FD. In his new position Hanson had responsibility for overseeing the Company's compliance with Regulation FD."

"This should be a wake-up call." notes Thompson in a NIRI Executive alert, "for all IROs corporate counsel and other senior executives." NIRI has long advocated—well before Regulation FD—that companies maintain a written disclosure policy.

This kind of question demands, on the one hand, the considered judgment of the CEO or CFO, aided by the company's attorney and investor relations officer. On the other hand, even within the bounds of flexibility defined by specific circumstances, it rapidly becomes clear that the body of law, no matter how new, no matter how large, no matter how complex, steers corporate management to frank, open and timely disclosure.

Insider Information

An *insider* is generally defined as anyone who has material information about a company that has not been publicly disclosed. It's assumed that any insider who trades on material, non-public information in buying or selling stock to his own advantage thereby functions to the disadvantage of other investors. Recent cases on both insider information and other categories of misuse of non-public material information, such as in the ImClone matter, have resulted in many a Saville Row suit being exchanged for prison garb.

A typical example of insider information abuse is the successful prosecution of Sam Wachsel, the CEO of *ImClone Corporation*. Upon learning that the U.S. Food and Drug Administration was not going to approve his company's application for a pharmaceutical cure for cancer, he sold his stock before the general investing public has access to that information. This kind of behavior—insider trading— says the SEC, is not only unfair in its own right, but causes investors to lose faith in the integrity of the market, by recognizing that those with informational advantages may exploit them and be rewarded, while others must rely on hard work and insight not derived from inside information.

In 1964, the problem of inside information dramatically came to the public's attention with the classic *Texas Gulf Sulphur* case. Several engineers working for *Texas Gulf Sulphur* came upon a rich mineral body. This discovery was kept within a small group inside the company. Several members of that group, taking advantage of their inside information and with full knowledge that the value of the company stock would be greatly enhanced when that information was generally known, purchased *Texas Gulf Sulphur* stock for their own accounts. This resulted in civil charges against the offenders. The court said that insiders must either disclose the information, or abstain from trading on it until it is available to all investors. It also strengthened and clarified the law regarding inside information.

Shortly thereafter, several *Merrill Lynch* staff members were given reason to believe that a forthcoming financial statement for the *McDonnell Douglas Company* would show a sharp decline in earnings. Before this information was made public, advice to sell their stock was given to selected institutional clients, at the same time that other *Merrill Lynch* customers were being given a buy recommendation. When the information was ultimately made public, the price of the stock declined sharply. The SEC took a dim view of the fact that there had been specific benefit from inside information to a selected few, and once again penalties were imposed.

Perhaps the major category of misuse of information arose as a result of a 1980 Supreme Court decision dealing with a printer who, in 1977 and 1978, traded stock on information he got from a confidential financial document his company was printing.

The Justice Department case was that the printer who had been entrusted by his employers to print confidential documents regarding a prospective takeover, had defrauded the shareholders of the target company (who weren't aware of the proposed tender offer) by trading on that information. The Supreme Court exonerated the printer saying that he didn't have a duty to those shareholders, and that if you don't have a duty, you can't breach that duty.

However, in a dissenting opinion, Chief Justice Warren Burger said that what the printer had done was to misappropriate—Burger used the word *stole*—the information from his boss, the printing company. Thus arose what is now known as the *misappropriation* theory. As subsequent events showed, had the government been able to apply that concept, the printer's conviction might have been sustained.

In 1982, in a case in which several investment bankers had traded on inside information obtained from their employer *Morgan Stanley*, the government indicted on the *misappropriation* theory that had arisen from Burger's dissent. The investment bankers were convicted, and their conviction was upheld on appeal.

It was on the *misappropriation* theory that some of the most famous insider trading indictments were developed, including Winans, Levine, Boesky and Milken.

Subsequently, other cases substantially emphasized the SEC's willingness to prosecute under insider trading statutes. In one case Foster Winans, who wrote the important *Heard On The Street* column for the *Wall Street Journal*, was found to have fed information to selected brokers about material prior to its appearing in the column. Because *Heard On The Street* is the most popular column in the paper, and because many people trade on that information when the column appears, knowing what's to be in the column before it appears offers a great trading advantage. The court ruled that the information in the column, and the column itself, was proprietary—that it belonged to the *Wall Street Journal*. Winans was convicted for misappropriating the property of the *Wall Street Journal*.

In another famous case of recent tears, arbitrageur Ivan Boesky, highly regarded for his success in selecting companies about to be taken over in leveraged buyouts and other acquisition deals, was found to have been trading on inside information. Boesky and many of his associates, including some of the most respected names on Wall Street, were brought down by the revelation, and many were successfully indicted.

Probably nothing is so seductive to the investor as the idea of being privy to—and trading on—inside information. It seems so safe. But it's amazing how sophisticated the regulatory agencies are in seeking out and finding wrongdoing in trading practices, particularly in this electronic age. The jails are full of those who discovered too late the skills and enthusiasm of the SEC, in dealing with insider trading.

SAFE HARBOR LAW

Inherent in the investment decision is the ability to project the earnings potential of a company, and thereby to value its stock. The stock market is, after all, an auction market in which buyers and sellers buy and sell stock on the basis of their perceptions of a stock's ability to appreciate in value. The stock market is a perfect example of an arena in which different people perceive the same information differently. Regulation guarantees that all buyers and sellers start with the same information at the same time.

But until 1995, shareholders, disappointed with the projections of management that weren't met, would rush to sue. Ours is a litigious society, and when a corporation announced an expected earnings per share in the fore-seeable future, and then failed to meet that projection, that corporation was often sued for that failure by disgruntled shareholders. The result of that growing tendency to litigate had been to inhibit corporate managers from forecasting legitimate and useful projections of performance.

Recognizing this inhibition, Congress passed The Private Securities Litigation Reform Act of 1995—the *Safe Harbor Act.* The new law was developed to reduce frivolous law suits by raising the bar of evidence of fraudulent behavior, including routine filing of class action suits when stock price dropped precipitously.

The Act puts a greater burden on the plaintiff to prove a case of negli-gence in making profit projections. But more significantly, it clearly defines a forward-looking statement that, properly delineated, protects manage-ment from liability. Under the law, both written and oral statements must be identified as forward-looking, and accompanied by meaningful caution-ary statements identifying important factors that could cause actual results to differ materially from those projected in the statement.

The law defines a forward-looking statement as . . .

- A statement containing a projection of revenues, income (including loss), earnings (including loss) per share, capital expenditures, divi-dends, capital structure, or other financial items
- A statement of the plans and objectives of management for future oper-ations, including plans or objectives relating to the products or services of the issuer
- A statement of future economic performance, including any such state-ment contained in a discussion and analysis of financial condition by management, or in the results of operations included pursuant to the rules and regulations of the SEC
- Any statement underlying or relating to any statement described in the foregoing paragraphs
- Any report issued by an outside reviewer retained by an issuer, to the extent that the report assesses a forward-looking statement by the issuer
- A statement containing a projection or estimate of such other items as may be specified by rule or regulation of the SEC

As a result of this law, media releases and other communications to shareholders now routinely include a safe harbor disclaimer. Corporate management would be well advised to make the disclaimer universal and mandatory, and to include it in the annual report to shareholders.

MATERIAL INFORMATION

The SEC uses as its definition of *material* the Supreme Court decision in the 1976 case of *TSC Industries, Inc. v Northway Industries, Inc.* That decision said, "An omitted fact is material if there is a substantial likelihood that a reasonable investor would consider it important in making his or her investment decisions. Put another way, there must be a substantial likelihood that the disclosure of the omitted fact would have been viewed by the reasonable investor as having significantly altered the 'total mix' of information made available. Information is material if there is a substantial likelihood that a reasonable shareholder would consider it important in making an investment decision."

This definition may best be seen in a consent decree issued some time ago against *Investors Diversified Service, Inc.,* containing the following language, "Material inside information is any information about a company, or the market for the company's securities, which has come directly or indirectly from the company, and which has not been disclosed generally to the marketplace, the dissemination of which is likely to affect the market price of any of the company's securities or is likely to be considered important by reasonable investors, including reasonable speculative investors, in determining whether to trade in such securities."

Any material information by that definition must be disclosed immediately. There is some leeway given by both the SEC and the exchanges if disclosure puts the issuer at a competitive disadvantage, as long as you don't trade or leak it. While the kind of information that comes under that heading is impossible to list to the fullest extent, there are certainly some obvious activities that should always be reported ...

- Financial results for a period
- Changes in corporate structure of any magnitude
- Mergers or acquisitions. Here, as in other areas of negotiation, timing becomes sensitive, since premature disclosure can sometimes adversely affect such negotiations. It is now generally accepted, however, that such negotiations should be announced at any point at which there is any feeling by both parties that the negotiations will reach a successful con-

clusion. This can be a verbal agreement or a letter of intent. But more often it's when both parties agree in principle on the price and structure of the merger or acquisition. Certainly, failure to disclose the negotiations at the time a letter of intent is signed is potentially dangerous. But the time to disclose prior to the letter of intent is still an educated guess.

- Earnings forecasts or estimates, with *Safe Harbor* (The Private Securities Litigation Reform Act of 1995) provisions
- Exchange offer or tender offer
- Stock split or stock dividend, or any other significant change in capitalization
- Decision to make a public offering
- A substantial loan or changes in terms of loans
- Listing on an exchange
- Changes in accounting
- Management change
- Major new product introduction
- Opening or closing a plant of considerable size
- Amendment of corporate charter or bylaws
- Any information that legally requires special filing with the SEC. In this context, include any consequential information filed in the 8-K report filed with the SEC.
- Significant environmental or civil rights matters
- Decisions of regulatory bodies other than the SEC, such as the Interstate Commerce Commission or the Federal Trade Commission.
- Material litigation
- Significant executive or board changes
- Rumors that may be damaging or too helpful

The list goes on and on, guided only by one's definition of material information for a particular company or industry.

FORM 8-K

The SEC also updated the disclosure items to be included in the Form 8-K, expanding two existing Form 8-K disclosure items, and transferring to Form 8-K two disclosure items that previously were required to be in companies' annual and quarterly reports.

Under the rules, companies must include disclosure about the following new items...

- Entry into a material agreement not made in the ordinary course of business
- Termination of a material agreement not made in the ordinary course of business
- Creation of a material, direct financial obligation or a material obligation under an off-balance sheet arrangement
- Triggering events that accelerate or increase a material, direct financial obligation or a material obligation under an off-balance sheet arrangement
- Material costs associated with exit or disposal activities
- Material impairments
- Non-reliance on previously issued financial statements or a related audit report or completed interim review (restatements)
- Notice of delisting or failure to satisfy a continued listing rule or standard, or transfer of listing

According to SEC staff, the final rules provide more precise triggers for the new disclosure requirements than the proposed rules provided. However, based on the SEC's discussion of the rules at its open meeting, and particularly in light of the Safe Harbor that the SEC adopted, it doesn't appear that the SEC is establishing objective standards of materiality. Thus, it will be important to assess carefully the actual text of the disclosure items once the final rules release is published.

In addition, companies must include disclosure about two items that previously were required to be disclosed in companies' annual and quarterly reports:

- Unregistered sales of equity securities by the company
- Material modifications to rights of holders of the company's securities.

The rules expand the existing Form 8-K item that requires disclosure about the resignation of a director to also require disclosure regarding the departure of a director for reasons other than a disagreement or removal for cause, the appointment or departure of a principal officer, and the election of directors. The rules also combine the existing Form 8-K item regarding a change in a company's fiscal year with a new requirement to disclose any material amendment to a company's articles of incorporation or bylaws. Other Form 8-K disclosure items, such as consummation of a merger or disclosure of financial information for a completed fiscal quarter or year, remain in place.

According to SEC staff, the rules don't include the proposed requirement that companies provide in Form 8-K a "discussion of management's analysis" of the effect of certain events on the company. The staff emphasized, however, that companies continue to have obligations under Securities Exchange Act of 1934 ("Exchange Act") Rules 12b-20 and 10b-5 to disclose any additional information necessary to make required disclosures not misleading.

The rules also shorten the filing deadline for Form 8-K to four business days after an event triggering the disclosure requirements. Under previous rules, the filing deadline for most items was five business days or 15 calendar days, depending on the nature of the event. The final rules do not provide for extension of the filing deadline for the new items.

CORPORATE DISCLOSURE POLICY

Circumstance and good sense suggests that the first order of corporate business, these days, is the promulgation of a corporate disclosure policy. Certainly, good management dictates a measure of contingency planning in all areas of potential surprise. NIRI, in its Standards of Practice For Investor Relations, not only advocates the policy, but also gives its members a sample policy.

Noting that no policy can serve all companies, NIRI urges that the policy reflect the company's disclosure position and practice within the guidelines of regulations, that the company assure that all members of management understand and agree with it, and that it be realistic within the purview of company structure and practice.

The NIRI sample policy gives, as examples of the kinds of material information that might come under the purview of disclosure, such factors as . . .

- Announcement of earnings or losses.
- A change in earnings or forecasted earnings that is higher or lower than the forecast.
- The launch of a new product or business.
- A pending or prospective merger, acquisition or tender offer.
- The sale of significant assets or a significant subsidiary.

- The gain or loss of a substantial customer or supplier.
- Major changes in senior management.

Obviously, this is only a suggested list. The range of corporate activities in today's business world is much broader than can be delineated here.

Unfortunately, securities regulation is not only complex, it's not always completely clear. There are many areas in which judgment must be exercised, as for example, the moment at which prospective mergers become likely and must be disclosed. The question of materiality is not an easy one, because what is material for one company may not be for another. Since these judgments are invariably made within the framework of regulation, and are interpreted by a wide variety of regulatory and judicial decisions in different jurisdictions that sometimes disagree with one another, there is clearly need for the professional assistance of a competent securities attorney, and the consideration of an experienced investor relations professional.

The primary responsibility for complying with disclosure regulation, however, remains with the corporation's management, with the assistance of its attorneys (not the other way around). In the realm of disclosure communication, the responsibility resides with the investor relations officer, whose skills and expertise are largely predicated on communication to the investment community.

It may be useful to note here the difference in viewpoints that frequently arise between attorneys and investor relations consultants. The attorney, charged primarily with being able to defend his or her client to the point of walking into court "with clean hands", frequently takes positions that are extremely defensive. The investor relations consultant, on the other hand, is charged with keeping the client viable in the marketplace, which means outreach and communication. The points of view frequently conflict. It's well worth the effort, though, for management, its securities counsel and the investor relations professional to work together and respect one another's constraints. Each has a distinct point of view and experience to offer, and the position of each must be given due consideration.

MOSAIC INFORMATION

Analysts frequently piece together a picture of a company's financial position and future by pulling together information from a number of sources, other than direct contact with the company, from their own knowledge of the company, its management, and its industry. NIRI points out that while this kind analysis is valuable, and that the SEC says that FD is not intended to discourage discussions between companies and analysts on the basis of nonmaterial information or material information that's public, a company is under no obligation to confirm or deny an analyst's conclusions arrived at in this way.

THE QUIET PERIOD

Companies often choose to maintain a quiet period, during which they won't comment on earnings guidance or prospects. NIRI notes that a quiet period helps shield a company from commenting on earnings information beginning when it has a more firm idea of the quarter's earnings and until the final earnings are publicly announced.

DISCLOSURE PHILOSOPHY

Speaking before a joint meeting with the Association For Investment Management and Research, the organization of security analysts (now called the Chartered Financial Analysts Federation), NIRI's Lou Thompson noted that "From a purely legal point of view, a publicly held company is only obligated to comply with the SEC's filing requirements. They are not obligated to talk with anyone." However, he points out, "... companies with a more open disclosure policy experience lower stock price volatility, a tighter range of earnings estimates, and a lower cost of capital. Subsequent disclosure research clearly supports these conclusions."

Because the body of regulation regarding disclosure is so elaborate, and so much of it is a question of judgment, much of the direction necessary to make those judgments is not codified. There are times when the SEC seems to be saying, in effect, "Do it first, and then we'll tell you whether you should have done it or not." While the ultimate judgment may depend heavily on attorneys' advice, the corporation and its investor relations professional should nevertheless adopt a basic philosophy that should pervade its disclosure program. This philosophy should be grounded in two key points...

Full Disclosure. The company should be prepared to disclose any and all information that could conceivably affect a judgment of an investor in the company as an investment vehicle. That is the ultimate rule. If there is any question—disclose. Certainly, this includes any activity that warrants filing a Form 8-K with the SEC, which is used between formal reporting periods to report significant changes in corporate activity, policy or practice. But that is not the sole guide.

Disclosure Timing. Pertinent or disclosable material information, such as earnings statements and dividends, should be processed for release as soon as possible from the time the information is known by any officer of the corporation. The machinery for disclosure should be well established beforehand, whether it's done by the company itself or through the auspices of the investor relations counsel. It should then be a routine matter to prepare and disseminate any information.

For many corporations, this kind of policy may seem harsh and arduous. But the balance must be sought between the basic responsibility to investors and potential investors on the one hand, and the value of competing in the capital markets by disseminating every element of information that materially assists in evaluating a company on the other. And while these two parallel goals may occasionally conflict, and there may be a temptation to hedge on the rules, it should be clearly understood that administration of the rules of disclosure can be rigid and assiduous. The SEC and the exchanges, it should be perfectly clear, mean exactly what they say. Furthermore, as understaffed as the SEC or any other regulatory body may be at any given moment, the agency is rarely lax in enforcing securities regulation.

And let's dispense immediately with any question of secrecy on the basis of competitive advantage. While the SEC has frequently said that it has no intention of putting any company at a competitive disadvantage, and will indeed allow competitive disadvantage as a defense in some cases, it still considers the dissemination of material information to be more important under the Rules of Disclosure. This can sometimes raise thorny points for a corporation asked to break down its performance by product line or by division, or for the corporation that feels that premature disclosure of merger negotiations might adversely affect those negotiations. Here, competent legal counsel is essential.

Furthermore, to the extent that individual and presumably unsophisticated investors are in the market, the SEC is increasingly concerned with protecting those investors. Purely and simply, the SEC wants no investor or prospective investor ever put in the position of buying, holding, or selling stock on the basis of incomplete or inaccurate information. The drive is toward greater and greater disclosure, however painful this may appear to be to corporations, or however time consuming this may be to corporate officers.

What is clear, under both the letter and spirit of the new laws and regulations, is that relations with investors are in transition. Where once the corporation's perceptions of its own needs were paramount (if not always accurately perceived), now the investor is at the core, and the needs of the investor for the information and tools to make considered investment decisions are paramount. Corporate democracy, like political democracy, may have its difficulties, but ultimately, it pays. To the company that recognizes that it must compete for capital over the long run, the problem of disclosure should be viewed not only as one of regulation, but as the opportunity to display every aspect of the company that can contribute to a rounded picture for the prospective investor or lender.

THE DISCLOSURE VEHICLES

In recent years, exploding technology and innovation have created new media that enhance the distribution of news and other information to investors. Communications vehicles that were either non-existent or novelties just a few years ago are now standard. The fax machine, for example, only a decade or so ago touted as state-of-the-art, has been largely replaced by e-mail. The web site, once an interesting tool for computer hobbyists, is now a serious vehicle for corporate communication. It would be difficult to find a company of any size today that doesn't have its own web site. The corporate web site is now a standard and ubiquitous operating tool, used for customers, suppliers, and investor relations

Many companies now have intranets—web sites used solely to communicate internally. Increasingly, companies are tying their intranet sites with one another in *extranets*, allowing them to communicate vital relevant data to one another in real time.

The past few years have seen a dramatic increase in business news, particularly on the broadcast side. Business news on television, once limited to only a few moments of air time, is now a popular feature. Television now reports stock market averages throughout the day, and CNBC runs the stock tape on a real time basis. *Bloomberg*, the business news service that now competes with Dow Jones, now has a full time business radio station, and a television broadcast.

Any shareholder with a computer, which today means virtually every shareholder, can access company information online for the latest information, financial or otherwise, either directly from a company's web site, or through the online services, such as Yahoo or MSN. All filings of SEC mandated documents are now available, at no cost, on the SEC's web site, *www.sec.gov.*

In other words, we now live in an environment in which an investor's access to information about a company is ubiquitous. Moreover, most of the information is in real time—up-to-date by the minute, constantly accessible the moment it's available. This is a far cry from the frozen-by-date printed material. The printed financial statement that closes on December 31 at midnight is now superseded by the internet financial report of midnight plus one minute, if information there is at that time. Financial reports are no longer static—they can be dynamic.

The effect of this dynamic, real time information on the securities market is profound. Investment decisions are made based on more current information, and possibly faster than ever before. It may be difficult to know the extent to which this new information environment contributes to the burgeoning volume of trading, but certainly it affects it.

WHAT IS INFORMATION?

It may be useful to examine the meaning of information, particularly because information is the fuel of investor relations. Understanding that meaning is crucial to effectively communicating values in investor relations, where decisions are made based upon the quality of information.

First we know that *data* is not *information,* and information is not *knowledge. Data,* we know, are basic facts—unalloyed, with little or no value outside their own existence. To say, for example, that a tree is a tree merely defines that object. It says nothing of its structure, its purpose, its value. It tells us nothing about forests or forestry, or uses of its leaves or trunk. That a tree is a tree is *data,* not *information.*

Information integrates the existence of a tree with the existence of, say, furniture. Then the facts of a tree take on a new meaning.

Knowledge is taking the information about the tree and the furniture and using it to inform either forestry or furniture manufacture. *Knowl-*

edge management is codifying the knowledge and converting it to useful information.

WHAT IS KNOWLEDGE?

Theoretically, *knowledge* may be defined as information that is now, or may in the future, be useful in a specific context. Knowledge may also be abstract, with no immediate use or application, in which case it may serve as a foundation for an ultimate use. For example, when the laser was discovered in the AT&T labs a few decades ago, it was merely a scientific phenomenon, with no apparent practical use. The uses emerged and were developed much later.

In a business context, *knowledge* is information that can be applied for a specific and useful business purpose. For example, the demographics of a particular market area is raw *data*. Analyzing that data in terms of the ability to make decisions about serving that area is *information*. Knowing how to apply that information to make those decisions is *knowledge*. Knowing how to deliver knowledge to those who can use it most effectively to meet a specific objective is *knowledge management*.

Knowledge—*cognition,* in this context—has specific properties that must be understood if the subject is to have any practical value.

- *Knowledge is dynamic.* Its value and quality change constantly. An illustration of dynamic information is an *address in space.*

  For example, if someone asks where you live, the answer can be defined as a fixed position, say the corner of X and Y. That is a constant static point that was there yesterday, is here today, and is most likely to be here tomorrow.

  But if you ask for the address of a body in outer space, the answer is, *in relation to what?* Objects in space are in constant motion, and are located in relation to other objects in motion. This is dynamic motion. Knowledge is, in the same way, dynamic.

  Even with the common language needed for communication, we know that this dynamic must be recognized if knowledge is to be useful. Knowledge is subject to...
  - Changing sources of input
  - Changing input from the same sources
  - Changes precipitated by the use of knowledge
  - Changing needs for the same information or data

- *Knowledge is cumulative.* Nothing is often known by just one person—nor is it ever known in entirety. For example, what bits of knowledge did the Wright brothers bring together to make an airplane? Or Edison, Bell, or Morse, for their inventions?

  The same knowledge can serve different purposes. For example, an area's demographics may help the marketing department define the nature of a product. That same demographic information may help the finance department determine the cost of serving that market.

- *People process information differently.* This, of course, is the crux of the stock market—the auction market in which different people give different values to the same information. Each person receives information through a screen of personal experience and prior knowledge. Give two people the same information about a company and its investment potential, for example, and one will choose to buy the stock and the other to sell it.

- Another form of knowledge is *tacit knowledge*—what we know only intuitively, but can't test pragmatically. For example, Freud's view of infant perception and psychology could only be surmised, but not tested. But if we build a system predicated on that intuition, and the system works, then we may assume that the intuition may be valid.

- Merely accessing knowledge can change the nature and value of that knowledge. For example, accessing information about a company's stock can change the value of that information, both in the way it's perceived and in the way it's acted upon.

The practical application of these concepts is a function of context. Knowledge of itself is one thing to a philosopher, another to a scientist, another to an artist or writer or journalist, and another to a functioning business person or professional. Knowledge, and the effective communication of it, is crucial in investor relations.

This new communications environment certainly broadens the base of investors to whom the latest information about a company is crucial, and therefore adds its own urgency to timely disclosure. The breadth of the investor base may be greater than the depth of knowledge about how to make an investment decision, but the growth of the discount, no-frills, no research broker indicates that more and more investors are making their own investment decisions. Does this not increase the responsibility of the corporation to disclose all material information as widely as possible? And with greater timeliness?

From the point of view of investor relations, the new communications structure offers the opportunity to reach more investors and potential investors than ever before. From a marketing point of view, it affords the company the opportunity to broadcast its message to investors faster, more broadly, more accurately than was possible in the days when the printed word was the prime vehicle. It generates more informed, and therefore better, investors. If the new media are used wisely, the corporation benefits.

THE NEWS RELEASE

The news release to the financial press, the wire services, and the broadcast media is the primary legal tool of timely disclosure. It is the first line of timely disclosure. Not only are news releases prescribed for routine reporting, such as earnings, but they are essential for announcing any material event that might affect the evaluation of the company.

In the amorphous area of timely disclosure, there is the pervasive question of when material news is considered officially public. At one time it might have been a simple matter—when *Dow Jones* or *Reuters* had it, it was public. Then, with the advent of *PR Newswire* and *Business Wire*, it was assumed that the full text of the release would be in the hands of these key wire services within 15 minutes following release. Then came *Bloomberg News Service*, which became, with *Dow Jones* and *Reuters*, the third legally accepted full disclosure medium. Under the new regulations, distribution to these services is mandatory.

The conference call or Webcast, under certain conditions, can be construed to be public disclosure. The SEC has indicated that posting material information on the Web does not absolve the company from the obligation to distribute the news in the traditional way. Posting on the Web alone, then, is not sufficient disclosure under SEC rules.

The burgeoning of the computerized world has raised some new questions—and offered some new solutions. Internet. Web sites. Webcasting. News retrieval services. Simultaneous fax broadcast. Computer services, such as *AOL, MSN, Yahoo,* and *CompuServe.* All of these give investors instant access to financial news, and in most cases, do so on demand. No more waiting for *Dow Jones* or *Reuters* to run the news on their wires. No more waiting for the newspapers the next day. For the eager investor, and certainly for the investment professional, the news is available within minutes after release, and often minutes—sometimes hours—before the information is available through traditional sources.

Few corporations now mail the quarterly earnings release to shareholders. The information is readily available through electronic means, such as the company's Web site.

THE INTERNET

The internet is a magic carpet. It can carry a virtually unlimited amount of information about a company, and probably should. Unlike print media, which freeze information in time, any information on the company's web site can be easily changed on a moment's notice, and through e-mail, can be broadcast to vast numbers of investors. While it's not yet of itself qualified as a medium of full disclosure, any information that is disclosed to appropriate media belongs on a web site, and disbursed by e-mail.

CONFERENCE CALLS

Webcast conference calls have become one of the most widely used means to disseminate corporate information to investors. It's a way to inform and interact with large numbers of investors and others in the financial community. If the conference call is readily accessible to the public and non-exclusionary, Regulation FD accepts it as a vehicle for full and fair disclosure. Transcripts should be retained, and freely distributed after the event.

Participants in the call should be given several days notice, and for quarterly calls, at least a week. Should there be any unintentional disclosure of material information, in either the presentation or the question period, full disclosure to the media should be done as a follow up.

E-MAIL TO SHAREHOLDERS

E-mail to shareholders is sometimes a useful device to supplement timely disclosure releases to the media to advise shareholders of major events that affect the company. They are prescribed in those circumstances where special action must be taken, such as a merger that will ultimately require the approval of shareholders, and for which a proxy for a special meeting is forthcoming. They are also useful to amplify a news report, to clarify a serious rumor, or to share news of special import, and should be used more frequently than in the past. To a large extent, they've supplanted letters to shareholders. E-mails are not, however, considered to be vehicles of full public disclosure.

THE ANNUAL MEETING

The annual meeting is the official gathering of all shareholders to conduct the company's corporate business, and is the appropriate time and place to report on the past year's activities. It's also the time at which the annual "state of the company" address is given, and the year to come is examined. But it must be realistically recognized that the annual meeting is rarely attended by any but the smallest portion of shareholders. It cannot be assumed that any announcement made solely at the annual meeting is proper dissemination of information. Any announcement of timely material information at the annual meeting should be followed immediately by a news release. Some annual meetings are now Webcast to reach a larger audience

ISSUER-PAID RESEARCH

A practice that had heretofore been fairly common is issuer-paid research, in which research reports are purchased by a company. While some of these reports have, in the past, clearly stated that they were not independent reports, too often the line has been crossed. NIRI has guidelines that say when analysts do paid reports, they must...

- Only accept cash compensation for their work, and must not accept any compensation on the content or conclusions or the resulting impact on share price.
- Disclose in the report...
  - The nature and extent of compensation received
  - The nature and extent of any personal, professional or financial relations they, their firm, or its parent, subsidiaries, etc. may have with the company.
  - Their credentials, including professional designations and experience, that qualify them to produce the report.

○ And any matters that could reasonably be expected to impair their objectivity in drafting the report.

On the company side, issuers must...

- Engage qualified analysts
- Pay for research in cash only
- Not attempt explicitly or implicitly to influence the research recommendations or pressure the analysts to produce research favorable to the company
- Ensure disclosures required of the analyst are included in the research report that is distributed whole or in part by the company.

THE SEC AND INVESTOR RELATIONS CONSULTANTS

Significantly, the SEC doesn't automatically exempt from its regulations agents of the corporation. For many years it was the practice of companies to use external investor relations consultants and public relations firms as mere conduits of information. Historically, corporate presidents relied on investor relations consultants to simply take the information supplied to them by the company, cast it into its appropriate release form, and disseminate it. Investor relations consultants, since they are seldom accountants or lawyers, are often without the full means or facility to judge the validity of information supplied to them. They once relied on their clients to supply them with complete and accurate information. Unfortunately, they were frequently fooled. For many years this rankled the SEC, and quite appropriately. The particular anxiety was that investor relations practitioners were unwittingly being used to *condition the market*—to unduly influence the market. In 1969, the SEC decided to include investor relations consultants in its regulation of disclosure.

Now, if appropriate systems and procedures to verify information are duly established and followed, and properly documented in the agency's own files, an investor relations consultancy has fulfilled its public responsibility and is not compelled to insure the total validity of the information.

The SEC takes into consideration the fact that investor relations practitioners, particularly independent consultants, are not in the same position to verify information as are auditors and attorneys. However, the investor relations consultant is entitled, and should be encouraged, to ask for documentation on any information supplied by the client. Steps can be taken to assure, within the limits of any investor relations firm, the most feasible precautions against dissemination of misleading or inaccurate information. They may vary from company to company, but essentially they rely upon documentation of instructions from client to counsel, with approval in writing for all releases.

COMPLIANCE PROCEDURE FOR INVESTOR RELATIONS FIRMS

A compliance procedure for practices by investor relations consultants in issuing information should be standard, and appropriate parts of the procedure should be disseminated to all clients. This protects both the company and the consultant, as well as the investing public. It assures that all issued information is carefully reviewed (and if necessary, questioned), and that all sources are clearly identified. And certainly, the consultant, for his or her own protection, should review carefully all available financial and corporate data and background on each of its prospective clients, to assure that it represents only reputable companies.

A primary factor in compliance procedures for investor relations consultants is that they know their clients. In a proper relationship, the consultant works closely with the chief executive and financial officers, and should come to know a great deal about them and the company. The consultant is well informed about the company's financial and corporate structures, as well as its day-to-day operations. This basic knowledge provides a framework in which to judge new financial and operational information, and should assure the consultant that he is not complicitous in disseminating false information. At the same time, the well-informed consultant may well be considered an insider, in that he or she has access to inside information. The consultant must function accordingly.

Proper compliance procedures for external consultants require that all issued material must be accompanied by an appropriate form, retained by the consultant, with a copy of the material, indicating the source of information, the time it was given for release, the time it is to be released, whether the copy has been or is to be amended, and by whom. Additional comments might indicate who prepared the original material, recommendations made by the consultant but not accepted or followed by the client, and how the information was transmitted for preparation for release. If additional approval is required or was given by attorneys, accountants, or others, it is indicated. The form is then signed by the company officer responsible, as well as by the consultant responsible. In the case of a release approved by telephone, or supplied by mail or fax, a variation of the form, designed for that purpose, is used, and signed by the consultant who received it.

Many consulting firms designate a senior firm member as compliance officer. The compliance officer's job is to oversee all procedures for compliance with SEC, exchange, NASD, *blue sky* regulations, and the firm's own policies, and should include a periodic review of all material and the ability to confer directly with the firm's securities attorney.

For the corporation intent upon disseminating false or misleading information, very little can be done by anybody to prevent it. Nevertheless, the acoustics of Wall Street are magnificent. The value to any corporation of issuing false information is remarkably short-lived, and the penalty, in terms of at least investor reaction, if not the law as well, is swift and intense.

EXCHANGES AND DISCLOSURE

The exchanges, while they control only listed companies, have been no less lax or intensive in their own drives for disclosure regulation. The New York Stock Exchange, recognizing the value of credibility in obtaining investor confidence, has a number of guidelines to increase corporate financial disclosure that parallel those promulgated by the SEC. The American Stock Exchange and NASDAQ have their own comparable disclosure regulations as well. NASDAQ revised its listed company disclosure rules to make them compatible with Regulation FD. In other words, every regulatory body concerned with the publicly held company is not only deadly earnest about fully disclosing information that's required to be disclosed, but is accelerating its drive to accomplish it and to increase those aspects of a company's operation to be disclosed.

It's important that copies of all material—releases, proxies and so on—be filed with any exchange or market on which the company is listed as soon as possible, before and after they are issued. Afterward, add the company's listing representative on the exchange and its specialist. For the over-the-counter company, add the market makers, after distribution. At the same time, it's important that while specialists or market makers be kept up to date on the company's business and trading activities, they should never be made privy to any material information about the company before it's made public. The specialist's posture must always be one of objectivity, and they could be seriously compromised by any inside information. Only in extremely sensitive cases, where an announcement might have significant effect on the market and on trading, will the exchanges and the NASDAQ want the material before it's released.

REGISTRATION FOR A PUBLIC ISSUE

One area of disclosure that can be difficult is the body of regulations that governs a company that has a public issue in registration. A company in registration is severely limited and prohibited from any activity that might be construed as offering, selling, or assisting in the sale of stock.

The basis for this regulation is the Securities Act of 1933, which prohibits offering or the sale of a security unless a registration statement has been filed with the SEC, or selling a security unless the registration statement has become effective. There are three periods of registration...

- There is the time before the registration statement has been filed.
- There is the period during which the registration statement is on file, but not yet effective.
- There is the period after the registration statement has become effective.

It's during the second period—when the company is in active registration review—that it's illegal to issue any material relating to the security, other than through the statutory prospectus. This is particularly true for an initial public offering. That second period is then clearly defined by the SEC as being "at least from the time an issuer reaches an understanding with a broker-dealer," and it ends with the completion of the dealer's prospectus delivery obligations. While the registration period is normally defined as 90 days for an initial public offering and 45 days for a secondary offering, completion may be considered by the SEC to be when the issue is completely sold by the underwriter. This situation is interpreted differently by various attorneys, and there is no consensus. Not included are the initial discussions or negotiations between the company and the underwriter. It's only when there is some form of commitment by the underwriter that the period actually begins in which the company is considered to be "in registration."

With an *initial public offering,* it's during this registration period that the corporation may take no action, nor issue any publicity, that can be construed as an effort to sell the stock or enhance the ultimate sale of the stock. And here, in view of other aspects of disclosure regulation, lies the paradox between what can and cannot be publicized. Material information will need to be discussed and added to the prospectus. However, if effectiveness of the prospectus is delayed, and an earnings statement is ready, the statement can and must be released. If the prospectus is already approved and the issue is selling, the earnings are released and prospectus is stickered by adding the information to the prospectus. Other forms of information that might affect the company and be construed as selling the stock, however, remain questionable regarding release.

ACCEPTABLE DISSEMINATION OF INFORMATION

The SEC recognizes the problem, and further accepts the fact that it's impossible to define in absolute detail those activities that a company in registration may or may not pursue. Each set of circumstances must rest on its own facts. Nevertheless, the SEC has issued seven categories of information that it deems not only acceptable during a public offering, but which it in fact encourages. They are...

- Continued advertising of products.
- Continued distribution of customary reports to stockholders.
- Continued publication of proxy statements.
- Continued announcements to the press of "factual business and financial developments."
- Answering unsolicited inquiries from shareholders, the press, and others (if the answers are responsive to the questions and prudently do not go beyond the bounds previously described).
- Answering unsolicited inquiries from the financial community.
- Continuing to hold stockholders meetings and answering stockholders inquiries at such meetings, without breaking new ground, unless information is disclosed in acceptable ways and added to the prospectus if necessary.

Obviously, the information disseminated under these seven categories should not include predictions, projections, forecasts, or opinions with respect to value. Nor should it include any attempt to describe the company in ways that might be considered promotional and supportive of a securities sales effort. And so once again we come to the question of judgment. And once again we come into a potential conflict between attorneys and investor relations consultants. Here, too, attorneys and investor relations consultants must consider one another's positions in light of the company's needs and responsibilities.

Without attempting to skirt or stretch the seven categories of information identified by the SEC, it should be recognized that not only is there tremendous latitude in the amount and kind of information that can be disseminated by a company in registration, but that both the need for and the value of such continued dissemination does not diminish.

THE SECONDARY OFFERING

The rules are perhaps more lenient during a *secondary offering*, but are otherwise the same as for an initial offering. Current shareholders must be kept informed, as in non-registration periods, and the company's stock must be supported in the marketplace. Subject to advice of legal counsel, it may be assumed that the same seven categories of dissemination apply, plus normal dissemination procedures. As with initial public offerings, projections of any kind that might be construed as selling the stock of the new issue must be avoided. This is a murky field, best navigated in conjunction with experienced securities lawyers.

There is also substantial value in an investor relations communications program begun well before the company goes into registration, in that such a preregistration program sets the tone for what may be deemed permissible while the company is actually in registration. On the other hand, there may be a problem if a company that has never communicated to the financial community suddenly begins such a program the minute it gets into registration. It's in this area that the experience of the investor relations consultant can be of exceptional value.

In the third stage, when the company is out of registration, all bounds are off for a financial communications program that's otherwise legal under any SEC regulations or sound business requirements.

In conforming to the disclosure regulations of the Securities and Exchange Commission and the exchanges, it's important to be thoughtful and considered. Premature and untutored disclosure may be even more harmful than no disclosure. You can't disclose piecemeal.

To avoid piecemeal or inadequate disclosure, consider whether you have all the facts needed to make disclosure, and then, if you don't have all the facts, you must ask whether disclosure will have a worse effect on the company than non-disclosure. The concern should be with not only the timing, but with the content of what's disclosed.

IN DEFENSE OF SARBANES-OXLEY

The very newness of Sarbanes-Oxley, and the revolutionary changes it's wrought, have visited upon the corporate world a great deal of anxiety, and even opposition. Yet, looking beyond the increased expense and labor, and the inconvenience, its passage has been salutary in the world of investor relations.

In an article in the *Wall Street Journal,* former Federal Reserve chairman Paul Volker and former SEC chairman Arthur Levitt Jr. put it most succinctly. They said, "Becoming a public company opens up a world of opportunity for a firm, but with that comes a responsibility to its shareholders. For too many years, too many people in and around our markets were shirking that responsibility, and shareholders suffered through investments made on bad information, restatements and bankruptcies. Sarbanes-Oxley was passed to reinforce the duties that directors, executives, auditors and others have to the investing public. It seeks to bring accountability back into the boardroom and executive suites."

CHAPTER 4

The Street

A Funny Thing Happened on the Way to Unbridled Wealth . . .

In the peculiar environment in which success seems to breed license, the booming success of the full cast of characters in Wall Street, during the boom years at the turn of this century, caused the Street to wake up one day to discover that their excess had been discovered. Congress, the SEC, and even the attorneys general of several states found that the traditional practices of Wall Street, particularly in securities analysis, investment banking, and mutual funds, had become tainted to a degree that might be considered odoriferous.

If the integrity upon which investors traditionally depended was safe in most quarters, it had clearly—and flagrantly—been eroded in some others.

The inventory of aberrant behavior was a catalog of dishonesty and dirty tricks, all designed to make everybody but the ordinary investor rich. Analysts pushing stocks they knew to be bad, but had been issued by the analysts' parent companies. Investment bankers allocating issues of initial public offerings to preferred customers before the general public was offered the shares at the issuing price. Mutual fund managers collecting fees for inflated or non-existent services. Accounting firms wearing blinders at audit engagements. And so on. It was a merry ride, before the government caught on and put a stop to it. In some cases, it meant jail terms.

But the foundation of the economy still rests to a large degree on a functioning stock market, and so changes were made. Firewalls were erected in investment banking and brokerage firms. New oversight structures were instigated. New regulations were promulgated, and the SEC was given new powers, new strength, new independence, and most importantly, new funds to do it all.

For the corporation that was *in on it,* there is now the burden of hewing to the straight and narrow. To the corporation already on that straight and narrow path, there's now an imperative to generate an atmosphere of trust that, if it does the right thing, and its investment bankers do the right thing, then the corporation and its shareholders will thrive. The honest corporate management—the one that can project that integrity—will compete effectively and successfully in the capital markets.

The academic view aside, how does it work in practice?

The stock market, remember, is an auction market. And since the stock market is an auction market, stock market prices don't increase in a one-to-one relationship to earnings. It's an exercise in mass psychology; in crowd psychology; in luck, and in a random action that has yet to be fully fathomed by the best minds. Still, the music of the myriad variables has been understood by some, and an increasing number of these variables have been tamed. A few. Unfortunately, not all.

It might be said, then, that a major role of investor relations is to reduce as many of these variables as possible, as a means to persuade the investor that the stock the investor relations professional represents will appreciate better than will another stock. Investor relations is indeed a competitive business.

But what really happens in this auction market is not simply establishing a relationship that assigns an equitable price to match the value—or even the earnings—of the company. What the market—and therefore, the professional investor—is really doing is not simply determining those companies in which the invested dollar will appreciate at a reasonable rate. The aggressive investor, and the advisors and analysts, are really trying to fathom which companies *the market,* in its collective wisdom, and driven by crowd psychology, will bet on to assign an ascending stock price.

In other words, the professional investor, or the securities analyst, or the investment advisor, in whatever role, must try to grasp, in a very practical context, a great deal of emotional reaction that's tempered by facts, half-facts, half-truths, rumors, guesses and in a few cases, shrewd judgment.

For the investor relations practitioner, this process is further complicated by the nature of *information* a word the meaning of which is mostly submerged, like an iceberg, and just as treacherous. (See the previous chapter.)

THE ANALYTIC PROCESS

Although technology now tends to blur the lines, and analysts tend to specialize in much more focused ways than before, the analytic process itself falls into two broad general categories—fundamental analysis and technical analysis. Today's market is too expansive and too specialized to reside heavily in one camp or another.

The *fundamental* analyst deals primarily with the tangible information about a company—its facts and figures—the chemistry, if you will, of a company—to which is added an assessment of how management will contribute to that company's success or failure.

The *technician,* or *chartist,* is concerned primarily not with the company, but with the stock itself, almost as an abstraction. The technician believes that stocks behave in a particular pattern that reflects what is known about a company, and that the pattern may be charted to project their future behavior. This behavior is divined by considering such elements as the history of a stock's movement, a statistical analysis of the market's behavior, volume, and so forth. By charting a stock's historical pattern, technicians believe they can project the pattern for the stock's future.

Naturally, there's a great deal of controversy among analysts and other observers of analysis about this approach. It can generate a great deal of heat.

There is, in fact, a great deal of peripheral viewing of fundamentals by technical analysts, deny it as they will, just as they tend to be persuaded by economic news. It is a battle of the witches of the East versus the witches of the West.

But there is a new factor now—the internet. As the computer, in its earlier years, altered the traditional methods of security analysis—massaging information—the internet has revolutionized the entire process. Essentially, with the internet, more can be known about a company by more people than ever before. As the internet has itself become more mature, and even institutionalized, it begins to put a new face on analysis, by both professionals and the individual investor.

In the mid 1990s, as the computer came into common use, it gave us a new kind of analysis—modeling. Its practitioners are quantitative analysts—or *quants,* as they're known on the Street. They function by building a computer model that relates every factor they think can affect a stock price, and then using the model to predict a stock performance. They frequently rely to a degree on classic fundamentals, but are more concerned with configurations and relationships of data. It enhanced the traditional analytic values espoused by Graham and Dodd in their classic book, and it brought the somewhat complex Modern Portfolio Theory (of which more further on), regression analysis, and even game theory, into the hands of even the mathematically challenged analyst and investor. All these theories, by the way, are a serious attempt to crack the code of whatever forces drive investors' behavior in the grand auction market. What it does achieve, in fact, is to help reduce the number of variables used to assess the future market value of a stock.

And what it has done, as well, is to change the nature of the analysts themselves.

But analysts, of any school of thought, whatever theory they cherish, are people too. They can be moved as easily by emotional reaction to the events of the day as are the most rank novices. Perhaps that's a good thing. If there were no diversity of opinion, there'd be no auction in the stock market.

It's certainly true that with the internet, the analyst and investor today have more information to use in analysis than ever before, and aided by the computer, that analysis, will be done faster and with more complex configurations and permutations than ever before. Moreover, the internet, by affording access to this information by the ordinary investor, an increasing number of investors have become their own analysts. Thus, the rise of the discount broker who need offer no service other than buying or selling stock. This is scarcely diminished by the fact that a number of investors, having stuck their toes in the waters of making their own decisions, are finding that it's not as easy as it looks. Many discount brokers have begun to offer, as a separate entity, research help.

These factors have, in the past few years, substantially changed the nature of analysis and who does it. It has, as well, obviously changed the nature of investor relations. If the market has changed, so too must the product change. And if competition has increased, then certainly delivery and packaging mechanisms must change as well.

Traditionally, analysis of stocks was primarily the concern of the research analyst—the descendent of the statistician whose job it was to analyze information, to come to a conclusion about a stock or the market itself, and to supply it to brokers, money managers, and others. There were perhaps a few diligent and seasoned brokers who did their own research, but only a few.

But today, driven in part by new technology and in part by regulatory changes, the distinctions between one traditional Wall Street role and another have been blurred. There are many more hands grasping for information than in the past, and fewer analysts function solely in that capacity. Aided by computers and other sources of information, people with many other roles to play in the market, as well as other needs for corporate investing information, are all participating in massaging information to make investment decisions. This includes brokers, money managers, individual investors, traders, institutional investors, investment and commercial bankers, and even venture capitalists. Venture capitalists, for example, tend to work closely with groups of investors for whom they supply a broad spectrum of investment ideas, primarily about early stage companies. Full due diligence, in which management is required to justify itself on many levels for investors, brokers, lenders and others, now goes much farther than merely a recitation of financial information, and demands at least as much as the traditional security analyst once demanded.

It should be noted, too, that a large measure of the demand for information is a result of the efficacy of the investor relations professional, who fostered the taste for more intensive analysis and due diligence by offering more information, as part of the competitive process for investor attention. Here, again, NIRI can take credit for educating both the investor relations professional, and the cast of characters on Wall Street.

One result of the changing dynamic of the Street is that where once the analyst analyzed and the broker sold, today many of both do both, and for a growing segment, the difference in their roles is represented more in shading than in distinct coloration.

The investor relations professional would do well to remember, as well, that no matter how immersed the analyst or investment professional may be in the esoterica of the stock market, it's all of the Wall Street cast that's either directly involved in selling stock, or is indirectly involved in the process as an analyst or advisor. It is, after all, a market. In a market, people buy and people sell.

An analyst was once asked, "What's the worst thing that could happen to an analyst who issues a research report? That nobody would buy the stock?"

"No," was the reply. "The worst thing is that the stock goes down."

What's the second worst thing that could happen? "That we recommend the stock and nobody buys it—and then it goes up."

For the investor relations professional, it's important to understand this concept, because clearly, the investor relations professional is part of the dynamic; is part of the marketing effort.

To the degree that we can separate each of the characters on Wall Street in this new environment from the Street's classic protective coloration, this essentially is what we find in each camp . . .

THE SECURITY ANALYST

It's difficult to view analysts as a group, and to draw too many generalizations about them. In 1971 there were 11,500 analysts. The exigencies of the stock market sharply diminished that number in 1974 to 10,000. It is almost reasonable—*almost reasonable*—to assume that those who survived the valleys of the business cycles of the past decade are all superb at their task. This is hardly so.

There are now more than 40,000 analysts practicing in the United States. They do continuing research on more than 2000 companies, with intense focus on only a basic 600—the group that comprises the majority of traded stock. As an example, in 1996, analysts at *Smith Barney* regularly covered 1,382 U.S. companies: *Merrill Lynch* regularly covered 1,140 companies; *Salomon Brothers* covered 1,147 companies; and *Goldman, Sachs* covered 1,081 companies. *Bear Stearns* covered 1,000 companies. *Robert Fleming* led the list, covering 4,122 companies. For the top 100 companies, there may be analysts dedicated to covering only one company.

Most analysts have a business school background and many have come up through the ranks of the securities industry. Ideally, the analyst has trained for the job in a context of new analytic techniques, and the new information vehicles. With the speed of information flows, and the growth and increasing complexity of the financial environment, today's analyst is to his predecessor as the jet pilot is to the World War I flying ace.

Analysts, like most people, tend to gravitate toward specialties. The specialists tend to form splinter groups and separate organizations. An analyst's interest in a specialty may change as investor interest changes. For example, there are many fewer steel analysts today than there were a decade or two away. Of the two general groups, those that specialize in types or size of companies and those who specialize in specific industries, interest shifts as the economy shifts. For a time, during the period of dot com failure in the early part of this century, there wasn't much for dot com specialists to do.

In fact, specialization tends to be a bit murky. For example, some analysts call themselves *special situations analysts*. This implies that they follow only companies that don't fit in other categories, and that portend vast improvement in both performance and the stock market. On the other hand, followers of the entrepreneurial company are specialists in a category called *emerging growth companies*. These are companies that are relatively immature, and yet give reason to believe—by virtue of their industries, their products or services, their management and markets, or other prospects—that they are going to grow at least 15 to 20% a year in revenues, and comparably in earnings. Sometimes, but not always, price/earnings ratio makes the difference, with the lower p/e companies addressed by the special situations analysts. At the same time, an emerging growth analyst might not follow a turnaround company, while a special situations analyst would. In many cases, it's more useful to think of *special situation* or *emerging growth* analysts as having preferences, instead of rigid categories.

As might be expected, there are *generalists* who follow any company they think will appreciate in value. But even among generalists, there are preferences. Some, for example, will not follow firms in a specific (and probably more complex) industry, such as energy or insurance. Sometimes, by the nature of the firm, the generalists follow everything. In the larger firm, with larger research departments, there may be greater segmentation and specialization. Beyond size and interest, there's also the question of talent and instinct. Analysts, remember, are people. They have idiosyncrasies and proclivities and instincts.

Industry analysts, specialize in one industry or another, not only out of their own interests, but because there may be greater market potential for the companies in that industry, and because of the complexity of the industry. It takes a great deal of time and effort to understand an industry's practices, language, distinctive financial and managerial structures, and nuances. At the same time, some analysts are particularly versatile, and specialize in more than one industry. And some industries may be related, such as oil and gas and mining.

Analysts' interests are often characterized by the firms they work for, each of which has its own market interests. Analysts who work for firms that are particularly retailers to the individual investor look for companies that are potential investments for the individual investor. These potential investments are companies that may be defined by size, float, trading reach, and so forth.

Among the scandals in the first years of the century were those caused by the relationship between brokers and their parent companies' investment banking clients, resulting in regulatory firewalls being established between the investment banking and the analytic and brokerage sides of a firm. The object was greater transparency in relationships between buyers and sellers, and between issuers and sellers, in order to reestablish and foster the sense of traditional integrity that had been lost by the scandals. Those in the investment community who had violated the traditional rules of transparency and integrity soon found themselves unemployed, if not in jail or forbidden to work in the securities industry. Most brokers are scrupulously honest and deeply concerned about their clients' assets, but there are still a few who are mere telephone pitchmen, and churners for commissions.

An analyst at a firm that serves institutions of money managers, on the other hand, is less likely to be concerned with companies with smaller floats, unless they see a potential for a company to grow rapidly.

These distinctions are not a hard and fast rule, but a general approach. However, because of the nature of the market today, with its heavy institutional involvement, the lines begin to blur. It's difficult to find a retail analyst, for example, whose work doesn't go to some institutions. More significantly, because the market is now heavily institutional, obviously the greatest volume of research is done for the institutional market, and most firms with strong research departments sell their research to institutions.

The point to be remembered is that analysts, even in groups, are individuals, and must be dealt with as such. To try to sell a camel to a horse trader is not worth the effort, unless there are no camel traders around. Pick your target thoughtfully.

THE BROKER

The stock broker is usually the direct contact between the customer—the investor—and the company whose stock is being sold. The stock broker, or registered representative, is primarily a middleman and a salesperson who has passed a relatively uncomplicated examination that determines an ability to understand the fundamentals of the securities industry. The broker's education beyond that need not be extensive, although some are highly sophisticated and skilled beyond their basic education.

Brokers work either on commissions or, in some cases, on a salary predicated upon a sales quota. It is perhaps this one fact that opens the spectrum of brokers' range of skills, motivations, and performance. More than any other group of financial or analytical specialist on Wall Street, the broker is the hardest to categorize.

Some brokers are pure salespeople who want nothing to do with investor relations professionals; some cherish the relationship. Some brokers rely only companies recommended by their own in-house research staff (although this is now done under the new regulations); some have full leeway. Some are required by their firms to get permission to recommend stocks not followed by their firms; others—particularly those with large clienteles—have greater latitude. There are brokers who are opportunists, selling the latest stock idea and then moving on to the next one, and there are thoughtful and responsible brokers, genuinely interested in meeting the investment objectives of their customers.

For the responsible investor relations professional who chooses to include brokers in the mix, the broker to be sought after is the one who is thoughtful, knowledgeable, understands research and how to do it, has a large and well established following, and is interested in good relations with good investor relations people not for the free lunch, but for the useful information. The others should be dealt with cautiously.

Traditionally, brokers rely upon their firm's research department for basic information about a company and for the intensive analysis necessary to make a sound judgment about a security, to which they frequently add information from other sources. More and more brokers are doing their own research, and some are getting very good at it. There are a number of brokers' organizations that serve as platforms for companies to make presentations, as analysts' organizations once did exclusively. The quality of these organizations, though, varies substantially.

Naturally, with brokers as the focal point for the customer, it's almost as important that brokers understand a corporation as do analysts, regardless of the degree of sophistication involved in that understanding. A knowledgeable and enthusiastic broker with a large following can place a substantial amount of stock, and some brokers form informal networks throughout the country with other brokers whose opinions they respect. Thus brokers are as important a target audience for corporate information as are analysts, if building a retail following is a goal.

Competition in the brokerage industry, enhanced by the elimination of fixed commissions, has also pervaded the discount stock on-line services, which have grown substantially through television and internet selling.

These firms offer no-frills buying and selling stocks at low commission, but with no research advice. But now the competition in the discount industry is being fought by adding the special services, such as research, that they originally eschewed.

Naturally, with brokers as the focal point for the customer, it's almost as important that brokers understand a corporation as do analysts, regardless of the degree of sophistication involved in that understanding. A knowledgeable and enthusiastic broker with a large following can place a substantial amount of stock, and some brokers form informal networks throughout the country with other brokers whose opinions they respect. Thus brokers are as important a target audience for corporate information as are analysts, if building a retail following is a goal.

More investors now make investment decisions based upon their own analysis. They then merely instruct the broker—usually a low fee, no-frills broker like *Charles Schwab*—to execute the order. They are more likely to come to the broker with the name of a stock they believe, for one reason or another, to be a good one. The low commission brokers usually don't give investment advice, but simply execute orders. The full service broker may inquire of his or her research department or simply give their own reaction to the idea, based upon knowledge and feelings they've gleaned from their own research. They are less likely than their discount colleagues to just execute the order without some comment.

The broker's job is the most precarious in the securities industry. Regardless of the general condition of the stock market, his or her job—and certainly income level—depends upon their customers' buying and selling stock. If the market is down generally and if the small investor is not investing, the average broker obviously does very little business. If the stocks the broker recommends, based on whatever factors, do not go up, or the stocks they recommend to be sold do go up after the sale, they lose their customers. Since it's relatively easy to become a broker, and extraordinarily difficult for a broker to make a good living in anything but a bull market, the turnover in brokers is overwhelming.

ON THE FLOOR—THE TRADER AND THE SPECIALIST

Old traditions die hard (some harder then others), particularly in the financial world.

With the vast number of shares traded every day on the stock exchanges, two traditional methods of trading are beginning to be obsolesced by technology, aided by some practices of which the regulators take a dim view. Two traditional roles in stock trading—the trader and the specialist—are very much in the regulators' sights.

Changes in the configuration of the market have altered and somewhat diminished the trader's role in some respects. As a buying force on the exchanges, the role, once powerful, has diminished. However, the power surviving with the trader is sufficient to allow us to look back upon the trader's previous influence with nothing less than pure awe. Years ago that job must have been even better than being a commercial banker. That was before NASDAQ became a major force - the electronic equivalent of a stock exchange without the venue of a physical location—and the heavy reliance upon the computer network for trading.

In the past, most good traders had substantial house funds available to allow active trading by taking positions in a stock (going long). Those were the days when information was scarce, spreads were erratic, and big profits could be made from smart trading. Now, with the computer, everybody knows everything immediately. NASDAQ, too, has siphoned off what were once the higher cap over-the-counter stocks. Spreads on the remaining OTC stocks are too narrow to make much money on active stocks, so traders widen the gap on lightly traded stocks to try to make more money there, and to compensate for the risks. The spreads, then, are too wide on inactive stocks. More brokerage houses, seeing diminishing chances to make money, are committing less money to over-the-counter (OTC) trading. OTC trading is being compacted into a business for some wholesalers who are growing, and may someday dominate the market. This may be compounded by the SEC reforms of over-the-counter trading, which can lead to a less competitive market with fewer participants. The brokerage firms themselves seem to be reluctant to bet their own money for their own accounts. Most of the trading now, and the reason for growth, is to service the growing demand by customers.

Are the traders the profit centers they used to be? It seems to be less likely than in the past, except for wholesale OTC houses that make virtually all of their money trading, primarily in smaller, lesser known companies—low cap stocks not big enough to be on NASDAQ.

At times, over-the-counter traders will still take positions in stocks they like in order to make an orderly market. However, these positions are not as strong as they were in the past. To the company involved, the size of the trader's long or short position can make a profound difference in the success or failure of the stock in the marketplace. A good company can have four to six market makers. A very popular stock may have fifteen market makers, but that's exceptional, and today, few stocks have that many.

Because of the losses that traders have sustained in the last few years, fewer traders will position stock these days. This reticence to take a position can make a mockery out of an orderly OTC market for the average small company. Short sellers can turn the mockery into shambles.

The best kind of trader to have supporting your stock is one who has a retail brokerage staff or institutional sales people in the company, because those salespeople can get some stock out at retail or with institutions. Increasingly, at firms other than the wholesalers, the trader is there to serve just the retail operation, and so is subject to pressure from brokers as to what stocks should be traded.

If the trader is with a wholesale operation, then he or she is generally just trading with other traders, and that can go on just so long, and the stock can go just so high, before some of that stock has to get out into the retail channel. There is certainly little impetus for traders to bid a price up among themselves in most instances. The SEC has been taking a dim view of this practice, and is moving to correct it.

Traders don't care whether the stock is going up or down, as long it is supplies volume. They work off the action. They get paid on the volume and on the spread, unless surprises, such as sudden swings, catch them on the wrong side of the market and there are some really severe losses. If they buy at $5 when the spread is $5 bid and $5.50 asked, they can sell at $5.50. If the stock goes to $4.75 to $5.25, they can still sell at $5.25 what they bought at $5. A sixteenth of a point is important to them. A quarter is a nice profit, on volume. If the market goes to $5, they might sell and break even, but that's a 10% move. And what if the stock rises?

These traders want to trade only *on the numbers*. They don't want to know anything about the stocks they're trading. They're going for just the small price changes, which is an art in itself, and they want to focus on that, and not concern themselves with what the company's actually doing. They're more concerned with who's trading what, and what positions they have, and making a profit on a very small price movement.

Their emphasis is on every minute that prices change, and where they put the spread, and how wide they make it, and when they mark the stock up an eighth or a quarter or sixteenth and when they don't over a specific period of time. Some of these decisions are based on the size and price of their positions. This is what creates a trading pattern and this is what makes the price go.

Frequently, the trader is armed with no more than the information required by securities regulation, which is little more than the company's most recent financial performance and filings. Most of the smaller trading firms don't maintain a research staff, and so the onus for keeping the trader informed must fall upon the corporation.

The younger, newer breed of traders are more likely to want to know about the companies whose stock they trade. They realize that it might help them to get a feel of where the stock might go, so that there's less chance for them to get caught on the wrong side. This is clearly a trend, and one on which investor relations professionals should capitalize. Get to know your market makers.

THE SPECIALIST

Equally important to the investor relations practitioner, however archaic the practice, is the specialist.

On the exchanges, the orderly market is presumably maintained by the specialist, a member of the exchange dedicated to buying or selling stock for his or her own account to balance and offset extreme swings in prices. But in today's technical and international era, the future of the specialist may well be obsolete. Until that time, though, the specialist has an important function in keeping an orderly market.

The specialist is an extraordinary figure in the financial world. Specialists are responsible solely for specific stocks. They use their own money, which means they can either make or lose a great deal, depending upon their judgment and the swings of the market on any given day.

A specialist tries to end each day as close to even as possible, which can't always be done. Millions of dollars are involved each day, and being a specialist can be as intense as being an OTC stock trader, or a commodities or options trader. While the specialist's primary function is to smooth the market by matching customers' buy and sell orders, there are many occasions each day in most stocks where matching orders don't exist. Then the specialist must step in and buy or sell for his or her own account. However, the specialist can buy more than required and build some inventory, or sell more than required and go short, depending upon the company and the current market action. This requires experience and judgment, and the ability to make several decisions almost simultaneously. When does a price move up or down and by how much? What price should a stock open at, given the book orders prior to opening? When should the specialist build an inventory, at what price and how much? Much of the specialist's role is governed by rules and regulations of the Exchange, but there are many instances when the specialist must step in on either side of a trade, quickly and surely, and turn a bad decision to a brilliant one. Like any other buyer or seller of stocks, the more the specialist knows about a company the better the decision may be, and that, of course, is the role of the investor relations practitioner.

Several specialist firms have been under suspicion for alleged trading violations, such as *front-running*—giving inferior stock-trade-executions quality to certain customers, including, sometimes, for their own accounts. These practices, combined with a potential for becoming obsolete due to new technology (which also makes around the clock, off the floor trading possible). Reorganization of the exchanges, begun in 2003, will undoubtedly see substantial changes in exchange trading practices.

Nevertheless, as long as the system still functions, specialists should be kept as well informed of a company's activities as should be analysts. There is no reason for a specialist to be surprised by the action of one of the companies he represents and protects on the floor of an exchange.

THE MONEY MANAGER AND INSTITUTIONAL PORTFOLIO MANAGER

A money manager oversees entire funds or segments of funds, both public and private.

The magnitude of large pools of capital requires infinitely more sophisticated management than ever before in the history of the capital markets. It also elevates the competition for attention to any individual security, and thereby demands greater sophistication in security analysis. When you consider the responsibility in managing multi-billion dollar funds in institutions, pension funds and 401(k) funds, mutual funds, high asset individuals and so forth, you can well imagine why money managers look to the broadest variety of analytical process available. And obviously, they cherish every bit of information about each company that can contribute to the analytical success. Money management is no longer a cottage industry.

The role of the money manager, in any category or specialty, has become increasingly important as the financial universe grows and becomes more complex. The vast influx of institutional funds, the growth of the 401(k), the increasing sophistication of investors and the influx of new investors, the proliferation of new analytic techniques, the increasing use of technology, and the internationalization of the capital markets—all have substantially altered the financial landscape in just the past few years alone. Also altered is the need for more advice and guidance for investors who are unskilled in managing their own investments, and the need for managers who can be trusted to invest to meet predetermined objectives. Thus, the burgeoning of the money manager, the portfolio manager, the mutual fund manager, the wrap account manager—in fact, more managers and experts per capita than ever before.

The title *money manager* is not cut and dried. In addition to the people who run the large funds, a money manager may be a portfolio manager, the head of a mutual fund, or a bank trust department, or a pension fund, or hedge fund, or a small pool of private investment capital, or a discretionary account for a brokerage firm. Some stock brokers manage money for individuals, IRAs, ESOPs, Keoghs, or even small institutions, such as non-profit organizations with small funds. More brokers are now listing themselves, even if without cachet, as *broker* and *portfolio manager.*

Fee-based asset management—the *wrap account*—has given rise to portfolio managers who develop portfolios of other managers, both stock and mutual fund. Their concern is not the stocks in a portfolio, but rather the investment and risk objectives of individual managers or funds. They are performance experts who manage large funds of money, usually from individuals, and who purchase the services of other funds or institutions. Some stockbrokers have developed clienteles for whom they perform this service, in addition to their classic brokerage activities.

Most money managers tend to use the basic research supplied by their own or other research departments, including research boutiques, to which they apply their own judgment. Money managers of smaller funds do more of their own research because they can be in positions where they have to make decisions quickly. They may not have the time to research an individual investment situation as completely as might an analyst. They do, however, combine instincts and training with reading and computer screening, and more and more, they meet with company management.

An increasing number of managers rely heavily on computerized models, and are concerned about information that can influence a decision, not general, nice-to-know news about the company. Their focus is on news that can affect their models.

Like brokers and analysts, money managers function in many different categories, each of which has different investment criteria. Money managers handling different portfolio sizes—$50 million and under; $50–100 million;

$100–250; $250 to $500 million; $500 million to $1 billion; and over $1 billion—will generally have some common characteristics. But beyond that, the investment criteria—objectives and risk parameters—for each group will change. This means, obviously, that the kinds of companies each category will attract differs. For example, a company with a market value of $100 million will certainly get a better hearing with money managers managing $250 million or less than it will from managers at the higher end of the spectrum.

Managing money, too, is a precarious job, since it is directly performance oriented, with very little margin for error. Thus the money manager tries to be as informed as possible in order to have a basis for judging the research factors. Increasingly, money management looks to objectives, whether mandated by ERISA *(Employees Retirement Income Security Act)* or by financial and marketing goals. Pension fund money is considered to have been managed prudently not simply when its asset value is increased, but when it meets predefined investment goals and criteria. This concept is becoming more ubiquitous in all money management. Thus, while the classic responsibility of the institutional portfolio manager—the person specifically responsible for the performance of all or part of the portfolio of securities for mutual funds, pension funds, banks, insurance companies, and so forth—is to choose securities that increase the value of the full portfolio, new criteria tend to mitigate performance measurements. And obviously, the more sophisticated hedge fund is a useful tool here, as well, for managing performance.

The parameters of each portfolio are very different one from the other. Some funds have portfolios that are passively managed, and drawn to match an index, such as the S&P 500. Some portfolios are actively managed, and chosen for growth, some for rapid appreciation, some for income. Mutual fund portfolios are most often highly specialized, and can be defined by an extraordinary number of different characteristics, such as risk parameters, industry group, geographic region, size or age of the companies within the portfolio, and so forth.

Funds are managed by fundamentalists, chartists, and subscribers to virtually every market theory ever promulgated, and are so identified in the fund's prospective.

This growing thicket of money managers poses an interesting problem for the investor relations practitioner trying to advocate a client's stock. There are no sure answers, but there are some rational approaches. For example, examining a portfolio will give some clues to the kinds of securities the portfolio manager might accept, keeping in mind that investment styles and practices may change rapidly, in response to a rapidly moving market. Managers' interests change as well. Certainly, talking to the manager will help. For a mutual fund, the prospectus defines the fund's parameters, but not the techniques used by its manager to select stocks. Obviously, index funds are exempt from the investor relations.

The best approach may be to use data from the myriad sources that have sprung up in recent years, as well as your own experience and contact list, to choose the fund that best suits the security, in terms of size, distribution, industry, etc. To best inform the institutional investor, examine the portfolio to determine the best approach to the manager.

This is further complicated, of course, by the fact that most portfolio management, like the market and the economy, is fairly dynamic, and parameters change as market conditions change. This means that to deal with any institutional portfolio manager, you have to keep checking.

VENTURE CAPITAL

A major source of investment capital is the venture capitalist, who, under quite precise circumstances, supplies the capital for startups, for early stage companies, or for established companies with growth potential.

The venture capitalist raises funds from a variety of sources that may include financial institutions, wealthy individual investors, corporations, and even the venture capitalists' own money. In return for their investment, they take a portion of the company's stock. The idea, in most cases, is to invest in a company that will grow, and either go public or be acquired, thereby providing the venture capitalist a realization of their investment in the company at a profit. In many cases, they supply management expertise and industry support. They perform an important service to the economy and to the emerging companies in which they invest.

A somewhat typical venture capital firm—they are all different in the ways in which they operate, in the size of investments they make, the industries they serve, the size and kind of participation in the companies they finance, and the stage of the companies in which they invest—is the life sciences fund co-managed by David Marcus, of Boston-based VIMAC Ventures, LLC. Their life sciences fund specializes in emerging technologies in the health care field.

"We anticipate that it can take up to five years for an investment to pay off," says Marcus, "particularly because the products we typically invest in usually require clinical validation—a long process, but one with substantial rewards if successful. Our criteria for an investment is pretty stringent, based upon our expertise and experience."

To be considered a viable investment by his fund, he says, the company must have a product...

- For which there's both a need and a willingness of the market to buy
- That's based upon ownership of intellectual rights with no clear competition
- That's based on a technology platform capable of producing multiple products
- That's past proof-of-concept and ready for commercialization
- That offers no safety concern

"At the same time," Marcus says, "we won't fund basic research."

It was venture capitalists, remember, who financed and built the high tech industry, and are currently fueling the biotech industry.

PIPES

Growing in popularity as a source of investment capital—and in controversy—are PIPES (private investment in public equity).

A sum of private money is used to buy a stake in a public company in need of funds from sources other than a secondary public offering. That stake can be in common or preferred stock, convertible bonds, or warrants. The financial instrument is purchased at a discount, which gives the PIPE investors an interest in the company, and gives the company the additional capital it needs.

In an example reported by the *Wall Street Journal,* the chairman of a seller of manufactured housing was approached by a group of investors offering to lend his business millions of dollars. In return, the investors would get bonds that could be converted into common stock and a nice interest rate.

"We thought it was a smart thing to do," said the chairman. The company was able to borrow $65 million at about 2 percentage points less than it could otherwise have done.

PIPES, as private deals, are usually kept confidential, because this kind of transaction dilutes the stock by the big investors who have bought at a discount. In fact, when the shareholders in the manufactured housing company learned of the deal, the stock slid nearly 11 percent.

Clearly, PIPES pose an investor relations problem, and must be handled carefully. On the one hand, it helps a company with needed capital. On the other hand, by diluting the stock it hurts the other shareholders. This is a minefield that must be traversed gingerly, with the announcement of such an investment—necessary under the Rules of Disclosure—made precisely and carefully, and with the flow of information carefully monitored.

THE CORPORATE PORTFOLIO MANAGER

The corporate portfolio manager's responsibilities to manage a corporation's investments of its surplus cash (other than the corporate financial officer's cash management responsibilities) now include being responsible for the firm's pension fund investments as well.

Most larger corporations, with cash surpluses, maintain extensive portfolios of stocks, bonds, and money market instruments as part of their cash management programs. Companies in the Fortune 500 are those in that category, for the most part. Some firms, such as *GE,* even use their surpluses as venture capital funds.

But today the corporate portfolio manager, under ERISA, has extraordinary fiduciary responsibilities. There are vast sums involved, even for smaller companies.

While most corporations depend on outside sources for advice, and even to manage the money in the pension fund itself, the corporate portfolio manager still participates in making final stock purchasing decisions.

These potential investors are not to be overlooked in your investor relations program.

OTHER INVESTMENT OFFICERS

Two groups that have grown in importance in recent years, with greater responsibility for investment decisions, are bank trust officers and insurance company investment officers. For example, *Northern Trust Bank* in Chicago sent a security analyst to examine a local mid-cap Chicago area company as a possible investment for some of the trust accounts for which it has discretionary authority.

Here, too, ERISA is largely responsible for these groups' increasing role in investment decisions. Prior to ERISA, trust investment, and much insurance investment, was limited to state-approved lists of investments. ERISA, which is the first federal trust law, does not limit investments by list. Rather, it responds to the Prudent Man Rule with much greater reliance on the investment officer to make decisions. The Prudent Man Rule, incidentally, says that fiduciaries must invest funds under trust "... as would a prudent man with his own funds." Under ERISA, the concept of prudence is fulfilled by adherence to investment goals, rather than to approved lists of investments.

OTHER ANALYTICAL TARGETS

Those segments of the financial community that have been described so far constitute the main body of specialists to whom the elements of a company's potential must be communicated. Naturally, nothing in this area is monolithic. While the bulk of investment decisions rest with analysts, brokers, money managers, and others, there are still fragments of the securities industry where opinions and impressions are important. For example, more individual investors than ever before rely on the vast array of information on the internet, making their own investment decisions.

There is value in having the heads of the corporate finance departments of brokerage or investment banking firms be aware of a company's profile, since they are frequently people who are sufficiently respected within their own company to have their judgment considered.

The role of the commercial bank in investing is growing rapidly, since the demise of the Glass-Steagall Act that had kept them out of investing since the 1930s. Bank investment officers are becoming increasingly sophisticated, a fact which is recognized by a growing number of individuals and pension funds that put money under management with the banks.

The person in charge of mergers and acquisitions for an investment banking firm is frequently looked upon as a source of new investment ideas, since the nature of his or her work brings the M&A specialist into exploratory situations with a great many companies. Within this context the merger and acquisition specialist has another interesting potential value. A merger is a form of investment of corporate assets. The mergers and acquisitions specialists can frequently put corporate information to better use on behalf of a corporation than can many other people in the investment community. They must be particularly careful, though, not to trade on inside information—as anybody who reads the front pages should know very well.

THE OVERSEAS MARKET

Until relatively recently, the securities industry outside of the United States wasn't attuned to investor relations as we here know it. The way for Americans to go into Europe, for example, was through American investment bankers with branches or associates in Europe. Access was limited, and very few American firms Europeanized themselves enough to really make a dent in the market. *Paine Webber* might have been an exception, at least in London and Paris, but *Merrill Lynch* and most others made comparatively little impact in Europe. Investor relations professionals who went to Europe and worked through a few local firms fared much better, and maybe even have a little edge today. But the wheel has turned toward bringing European investor relations to a par with the way it's practiced in the United States.

Now, tremendous strides have been made in investor relations in Europe and elsewhere in the world. It's no longer true that the rest of the world is still generally behind the United States, and in many countries abroad, investor relations is now considerably more sophisticated than it had been. The gradual breakup of old club attitudes in the financial community in the United States allowed investor relations to develop. In Europe, the old school ties existed to a much greater degree than in America, to the detriment of the professional investor relations practice. But in Europe, too, the financial community is changing extensively. Such investor relations firms have made the grade in comparable professionalism, and England, at least, has a thriving investor relations profession.

The investment arena is very different in each country abroad. For example, in most countries there is no retail market as such. There are no individual investors as we know them, except in Japan, which is a market very much controlled by the largest Japanese brokerage firms. England is just beginning to develop a retail market. You must work, primarily, with institutional investors or very large individual investors through intermediaries. In London private client brokers work with the investments of extremely wealthy individuals in Europe.

Since the deregulation of the British securities industry in 1986, it has undergone a vast readjustment. From the rush of the first days of deregulation—the *Big Bang*, as it was known—the industry moved to a high, then a low of disorganization, volume and business. It seems now to be stabilizing. The securities industries of all European countries are adjusting to a new context as the borders between European Community countries have fallen, allowing a new era in international trade.

For the U.S. company seeking to sell stock abroad, there are some major considerations, not the least of which is in the relationships that exist between the corporation and the different European financial markets. Different legal and regulatory frameworks also exist from country to country, although they almost universally subscribe to the same rule of disclosure that obtains here—that potentially price sensitive information be released as soon as possible. Accounting standards and principles differ from one country to another, making international analysis difficult, although this problem is slowly mitigating.

The financial press in Europe, for example, is truly national in each of the major markets, and is more influential, in most countries, than it is in the United States. According to European experts, a symbiotic relationship exists between the press, stock brokering, sell-side analysts, and investing institutions. The press and sell-side analysts trade stories with each other, and in turn, influence institutional investors. This is particularly evident, the experts say, during mergers and acquisitions, where the importance of the press is at its most obvious. There still tends to be some skepticism about investor relations, particularly among British institutional managers, but that seems to be mitigating as the results of effective investor relations efforts begin to emerge.

It's important, then, that American companies and their investor relations counsels functioning in European and Asian markets fully understand the workings of the financial communities in each of the countries in which they may choose to operate.

Identifying target stockholders should be the starting point of any program, and working with local sources is mandatory. This can be difficult, because there's no legal requirement to disclose foreign shareholdings. Moreover, in countries such as Switzerland, Germany and France, obsessive secrecy prevails, making shareholder identification doubly difficult. For larger American companies, for whom three to five percent of their stock is in foreign hands, the job becomes a bit simpler, since the shareholders abroad are usually on the company's lists.

It becomes clear that establishing relationships with overseas financial markets is a task that requires ongoing commitment. It's not a casual exercise. Nevertheless, it's important for the growing American company, because Europe and the Orient are sources of capital that can't be ignored.

WALL STREET AND BROADWAY

Wall Street and Broadway have one thing in common—they are both real places, and they are both a state of mind.

In fact, there are times that the drama on Wall Street is greater than on Broadway. And you can love and hate them both at the same time.

But just as on Broadway, if you're part of the dynamic, you have to understand the Street's operations, and you have to know the cast of characters. The roles played by the cast of characters are determined by one thing—go where the quality money is.

CHAPTER 5

Talking to the Financial Community and the Shareholder

Let Me Tell You About Our Company...

The changes, in recent years, in the structure of the analytic and investment community have been both profound and subtle. The degree of importance once given to the well-worn but often wasteful luncheon meeting, for example, at which there were sometimes a few serious analysts among those looking up occasionally from their plates to ask irrelevant questions to please clients or corporate masters, is now, it seems an anachronism. The loaded cannon of regulation, technology and the new forms of communication, and the extremely delicate balance and urgency of the competitive market, have shot down most of the sloppy practices of the past. The analysts that remain are mostly serious men and women with no time for anything but facts, and the framework of the new regulatory structure seems to be working well to keep analysts focused. The pain of scandal has excised the worst part of the past. Unless the tide turns again, the new breed of analysts may be deemed to be well on the side of the investor.

And the format has changed, particularly for the busier, more serious analyst. For example, there may not be the leisurely lunch meetings of the past, but there are highly focused web casts that impart the same information—and often more of it.

There are still meetings between management and analysts—but they are more often one-on-one, and the analysts given the time are usually people who have done their homework, who ask cogent and intelligent questions, and who have serious purpose. Despite the Schering-Plough situation, which raised questions about the efficacy of one-on-one meetings, these meetings should continue, as long as any material information revealed is properly disclosed to the public. What's good for some managers (and perhaps bad for some) is that analysts today are not easily fooled. In today's electronics environment, and with all the sophisticated sources, the acoustics are magnificent, and spinning ain't easy. It's certainly not profitable.

Looking at the picture in sharper focus, we see an interesting paradox. The larger company, with a significant share of its market, a larger stock float, and a heavily traded stock, has the broader canvas on which to paint its story. It's the smaller company, the one with smaller capitalization, smaller float, lower trading volume, that has to find the few analysts that can be persuaded to follow its stock, much less recommend it.

For the large cap and the small cap companies, it's a difference in the same thing. And so is the strategy different. Simply put, the larger company is more likely to benefit from the larger meetings, whether electronically or at a luncheon presentation. The smaller cap company may get enough analysts to fill a table, but might be better off finding and targeting a few champions. And of course, both benefit from meetings on conference calls.

A significant factor in straightening and narrowing the path are the regulations, such as Sarbanes-Oxley, FD and Safe Harbor. As a result, the softness has been seeping from the information pool, as the competition for capital becomes keener.

What, then, are the investor relations professional and the corporate manager to do in coping with this army of information hungry investors and investment advisors?

The answer is to stick to principles. Understand the process. And if it's there in the first place, take the management ego out of the mix. The personality cult of the trophy CEO has lost its currency in the market place.

There are may be a finite number of vehicles to communicate the values of investing in your company to the financial community, but each can be used artfully. For the analytical, institutional and money management community, for example, there are . . .

- The webcast
- The web site
- The conference call
- Meeting with or talking to individual analysts
- Talking to individual investors

- Meeting with stockbrokers
- Meeting with money manager or institutional investors and analysts
- Establishing relationships with portfolio managers
- Trader and specialist meetings
- Issuing supporting material, such as a corporate profile
- Electronic conferencing
- Talking to individual investors
- The annual report and the annual meeting
- Responding to unsolicited inquiries
- Additional printed material, including annual and quarterly 8K reports, distributed to the financial community and shareholders
- Regular and periodic mailing of information about the company to the financial community, including copies of news releases.
- News releases and features in the financial media.
- Corporate advertising and other promotional devices.

These devices cannot be allowed to serve as a conduit for irrelevant information, but rather should serve to meet a singular objective—*to persuade investors and analysts that a dollar invested in your company will increase in value faster and more substantially than a dollar invested in another company.* Every one of these devices is a prime vehicle to establish intellectual and business relationships with investors and those who advise them.

And remember, any material information imparted to individuals or groups, whether deliberately or inadvertently, must be released with dispatch to the general public, in accordance with Regulation FD.

Any meeting or contact that doesn't address that objective is a waste of time. Any meeting or contact that doesn't foster and move forward the company's position uses the time and contact badly. If there is no education, no enhanced understanding, no persuasion about the company—then the meeting or contact is an exercise in futility.

Nor can analyst meetings be mere image sessions, in which symbols are manipulated to present a picture of the company based upon fluff, and not reality. While the professional investor relations specialist can focus on the more cogent aspects of a company, no one can present a poorly run company as a paragon of management virtue, and long sustain that picture.

All financial community contact, then, should begin with a clearly defined objective. That objective might well be the answer to the question,

"What do we want them to know, think, or feel about our company after they've met with us?"

With that objective defined, the rest is mechanics. But the mechanics are important to successful investor relations.

Given an investor relations strategy, the mechanics consist of...

- Defining the position—the focused message to be conveyed
- Selecting the target audiences (groups of analysts, brokers, individual investors, etc.) and the key individuals with each group
- Determining how the message is to be conveyed
- Preparing the appropriate materials (presentations, documents, kits, visuals, and so forth)
- Arranging for the meeting and running it
- Following up

TALKING TO ANALYSTS AND INVESTORS

In view of the focus on professionalism, and the regulatory spotlight shining on them, analysts today are more likely to be more hard-nosed professionals than ever before. In talking to management, there is greater focus on getting to the information quickly and wasting little time on frills. There are several reasons for this...

- Analysts and money managers have more options for getting more detailed information. There is more broadcast information, the internet, faster and more accurate electronic information. Quicker and easier access to company information from the government (e.g. *www.sec.gov/edgar.shtml*), more audio and video teleconferencing, and company web sites. Analysts will come to the personal or group meeting better educated, seeking insights not otherwise available from other sources.
- Analysts and money managers have gotten better at their profession, and with Modern Portfolio Theory, regression analysis, computer modeling and other new techniques, and real time access to information, they are more sophisticated. They understand their special needs better.
- More companies are willing to see the analyst in the corporate office or at a neutral site for private meetings. Both sides now see the greater benefits in a private meeting even with Regulation FD in mind.

THE GROUP MEETING

Meeting with a group of analysts, whether in person or online, requires a different kind of structure, strategy, and even mindset, than meeting with individual analysts. The structure of the presentation for the group meeting is more formal, can involve other members of management, and incorporates the interplay of the analysts with both management and one another.

The group presentation should begin with a brief statement of what management believes to be the most important factors about the company, including its strengths and competitive advantages. An important part of the discussion should be to focus on the core idea that epitomizes why the company is an especially good investment—the position. If no other point is made but that core idea, then the presentation must be deemed a success.

If appropriate, management can delineate those problems that the company has had or that the industry has faced in very recent history, certainly within the past year. This is followed by an explanation of the company's long range strategies—it's plans to grow internally or by acquisition, or by developing new markets, it's new product strategy, and so forth. It then briefly describes the company as it's presently constituted—what it is, what it makes, how it distributes, the size of its markets, why it is in those markets. This is followed by a discussion of the company's financial structure. This leads to a discussion of management and plans for the company in the short term—the current quarter and the balance of the year. The meeting is then opened for questions.

Strategy statements and information about the company's future are the more important part of the meeting. There is no need to summarize key points, nor to go into financials in detail. Financial information should have been distributed before the meeting, and certainly before the presentation, and then the presentation can just touch necessary highlights.

It can be useful to talk to a few of the key analysts ahead of time, to fathom what they believe is important, and then use their direction as a guide to the substance of the presentation. Know your audience.

It's absolutely essential that no company executive attend an investors' meeting without having anticipated as many questions as possible that might be asked by the investment professionals, and having prepared a thoughtful and considered answer. Preparing the questions and briefing management is a crucial role of the investor relations professional. If the speaker doesn't know the answer to a question, he or she may refer it to another executive, or even the investor relations officer. For questions for which there's no immediate answer, there should be a prepared response, such as, "Give me your name and we'll get back to you with an answer by this afternoon (or tomorrow)." The most impressive presentation can be destroyed in a moment by one important question that's badly or hesitantly answered.

The tone of the presentation should be honest, forthright, and positive. Negative factors should be expressed clearly and in no way avoided, but they need not be dwelt upon inordinately and out of proportion to their importance to the overall picture. Hostile questions should be handled patiently and forthrightly and, even if the answer is negative in terms of the total presentation, should be ended on a positive note.

Don't let one negative questioner dominate the question and answer session. When there is a negative line of questioning, suggest that it can be followed up after the meeting is adjourned, so as not to bore the others who don't have a great deal of interest in the subject. However, you'd better be right in your assessment. The last thing you need is for three other participants to say, "No, we want to hear the answer too."

It should be recognized that despite all care taken in developing the invitation list, a certain number of investors will invariably show up who really don't care about the company, even if they discover that during the course of the presentation. They will seem uninterested or ask cursory questions. Not everyone present will see the company in the same way, nor with the same degree of sophistication. In any meeting of ten or more investors, there will almost invariably be three or four unimportant or irrelevant questions—questions asked because analysts feel they must say something to make their presence known or because they frankly don't understand something. These questions must be handled with the same patience as the more serious and delving ones.

The investor relations consultant or officer has a definite role, in the course of a meeting, to keep the meeting on track and to the point. That means shielding management from irrelevant questions by judiciously intercepting them before management answers, if possible; to help avoid confrontations by interceding as a mediator or clarifier; to deflect duplicate answers by gently interrupting; to avoid misunderstandings or direct attacks, and so forth. While the consultant or officer should not be obvious in a meeting, he or she should be an active participant, when it's appropriate and when rapport with management permits.

USING VISUAL AIDS

A great many company stories are well told by visual presentations—a short film, video, or PowerPoint slide presentation. This can be useful and effective if it's carefully done, in visualizing product and service, as well as in the graphic presentation of complex financial material.

The visual presentation, however, should never preclude a personal presentation by the chief executive officer. It should simply visualize that which is best visualized—the star performer should always be the corporate spokesperson.

Despite the fact that each person invited has been sent a kit of materials about the company, a duplicate kit should be placed on each seat before the luncheon. Many investors will have forgotten their kits, or there will have been substitutes to whom no kit was ever sent. Extra kits are usually welcomed. A potentially fatal mistake, incidentally, is to include a copy of the executive's presentation in the kit. There is nothing more distressing to a speaker than to look up and find ten or fifteen people following his words on the printed page, or reading ahead of him. It's good practice, on the other hand, to record the presentation and transcribe it for distribution to interested investors who didn't attend the meeting for one reason or another, or to pass it out or mail it after the meeting.

It's extremely important that every attendee of a meeting with analysts is contacted for a follow up discussion. The purpose is to get a reaction to the presentation, to determine each participant's interest in following the company, to build a following, and to reinforce the company's message.

INDIVIDUAL ANALYST MEETING

Depending upon your investor relations strategy, and the need to reach a specific group of investors, it can be worthwhile to take the initiative and target individual analysts. This assures that your target fits a profile of the analyst or institution within your chosen market group—the individual, institution or fund most likely to be responsive to the values of your company and its stock.

When you target an analyst, do your homework beforehand, and send ahead as much information in print about your company as possible. The point is to take advantage of the occasion of a meeting by devoting the time to helping the analyst understand management, its plans, its skills and capabilities. Why waste that valuable time on information that can be sent ahead? The meeting could be about a double check of facts, new factors and developments, new directions and to get to know management personally. Be prepared to talk competition, industry outlook and your strategy.

It's also an opportunity to establish a relationship with an analyst with access to important groups of investors—to build relationships for the future. Better analysts tend to be cautious, and make few snap decisions.

ELECTRONIC MEETINGS

Contemporary technology has opened some extraordinary avenues for communicating with large or selected groups of people at one time. And as with all technology, increasing use and technological advances have moved some of these techniques from science fiction to reasonably priced reality. It's now possible for an executive to hold a conference by phone, by video, by satellite, by internet, with an unlimited number of people in an unlimited number of locations. And it is literally a conference, with the same give and take to be found in an on-site conference.

The advantages, as with all contemporary technology, proliferate only to the limits of imagination. We know that we can hold the meeting or discussion electronically. But we are just beginning to see that the imaginative options are awesome.

The obvious advantages, of course, are the effective savings in time and costs. If you can talk to a hundred analysts throughout the country—throughout the world, in fact—at one time and sometimes on very short notice, and not have to transport either the audience or yourself to a fixed site, then you have more than the electronification of a formerly mechanical process. You have a new dimension in communication. If you can impart news to a hundred analysts throughout the universe at one time, and have questions asked from different parts of that universe, and shared at the same time with all of those people, then the news itself takes on a new meaning. If you can reach a large but selected group of analysts at one time, and have them participate in a discussion with management, you've built a broader but selected following.

If you're able to hold several meetings during the course of the year with large or selected groups of analysts in different locations, instead of only once or twice a year, you can develop a rapport based on an intensive distribution of news. It can take the news release much farther and more urgently than can mail or even newswire, can give you virtual real time feedback, and can keep you constantly in touch with the market for your securities. And all within a fraction of the cost of doing it in person.

Which is not to say that management and the investor relations professional are absolved from having to prepare carefully and intensively. The medium, in this instant, is not the message, and the content of the message must be the same as one would impart in individual or group meetings. The message is enhanced by delivering it more quickly and universally than ever before, and by getting a broader base of response and feedback than could be found in a smaller, local, meeting. The impact is at least more urgent, and through the effect of a broader spectrum of feedback from many different participants, can perhaps change the texture of the message.

Keep in mind that no matter what the medium, the message must go beyond merely imparting the numbers—*the metrics*. The ultimate objective of all meetings with the financial community is to project management skill and integrity. The numbers (with, perhaps, some help from management) speak for themselves. But the quality of management must be made clear in all public presentations. That's where the public view of integrity comes from, not from protestations and promises.

Electronic conferencing is useful. But personal contact, in most cases, is still best at building trust in management.

RUNNING THE ELECTRONIC CONFERENCE

Webcasts and teleconferences are relatively simple to set up, and can be done on very short notice, although notice there must be to avoid problems with Rules of Disclosure. They are, in effect, simply conference calls. Web sites give instant access to new and constantly updated information. E-mail is as ubiquitous as the telephone, and can be made secure.

The internet—and, therefore, the webcast or e-mail—reach around the world at no additional cost. The teleconference does not, except at great expense.

Video conferences, unlike teleconferencing and the internet, require fairly extensive preparation, and are best done by professionals. There is a question of equipment on both ends, as well as the graphics one would normally use in any visual medium. Expertise is essential here, and fortunately, there are a growing number of companies that do it. Competition in this field is breeding more realistic costs.

As with any mass communication activity, traditional or electronic, preparation must be meticulous. The planning should include at least the following steps as a guide, but not necessarily as fixed rules. Circumstances—and good imagination and skill—alter rules appropriately. The basics are...

- Determine the reason for the event, and its objective. The rules of the press conference apply. To hold an electronic event simply because it's possible to do it, or because it affords a broader audience, is scant reason. There should be a singular message, or at least a piece of news of magnitude, to impart; a realistic basis for urgency; a sound foundation for bringing a large group of investors together. The classic question to be addressed at this point is, again, *What do you want them to know, think or feel after the conference is over?*
- Determine the timing. Is each event discrete, and planned separately each time for a different audience? Is it a periodic event—quarterly, semi-annually or annually—to the same audience?
- Determine the target audience. Even though you can reach large groups at one time, you will still have a different message for analysts than for brokers; for analysts covering specific industries and for institutional money managers.
- Plan the invitation process. How will you invite people to participate? What is the timing of the invitations? What is the best response mechanism? E-mail? Fax? Mail? Phone?
- Detail and script the event. Who talks and says what? Who handles the questions from the audience? What material gets sent out beforehand, and what material afterward? What is the script to say and who is to write it? Do any of the speakers need training?
- Run the event. But rehearse, first. You're paying for the time, and the participants are paying with their time. Every moment should count.
- Follow up. How? With what? How often?

DETERMINE THE OBJECTIVE

While it might be tempting to use a teleconference or a video conference to simply replicate the classic analyst meeting, it might be more useful to use the event as a means to impart something specific and something more appropriate to the medium.

Obviously, differing factors dictate different approaches. A company that's new to a great many analysts and potential investors might want to hold and surpass the classic meeting, but the ultimate judgment lies in what could reasonably be expected as a result. If introducing an undervalued company to a great many potential investors is the objective, then the medium is used differently than it would be to tell a large group of analysts who have been following the company about the meaning of new products or new contracts.

One key to the success of an electronic conference is to recognize that, more than in the classic meeting, the level of focus and attention of participants can be exceptionally high. But that also means that the opportunity is best seized by focusing on a single message—a single position—for each conference. The answer to the question of what you want participants to know, think and feel afterward is a good starting point. While it's tempting to try to make more than a single point on your nickel, it just doesn't seem to work. One major point, reiterated and supported with facts, does work.

This assumes that you've done your homework in vetting the participants, and in sending ahead the kinds of facts and figures that participants can read and refer to at leisure, and that don't need to be reiterated in detail by management as part of the presentation. The facts and figures, remember, support the message. They should not be the message itself—unless, of course, the facts and figures are the point of the session.

DETERMINE THE TIMING

If you're using the conference to supplement disclosure, then the timing is dictated by the Rules of Disclosure. Webcasts and teleconferences are useful on short notice, when special events require quick follow-up to disclosure of the kind of urgent news that you are also putting in a news release, like a major acquisition, an unfairly negative news story, a fire at a major plant, and so forth. The quarterly webcast is becoming the standard for informing key investors and analysts in small groups, as well as larger groups, if circumstances warrant it. A mid-quarter teleconference is an excellent vehicle for new or potential investors who might not fully understand the company.

The time of day for a conference is dictated by the nature of the conference and the audience, remembering, again, that a webcast requires infinitely more preparation than does a teleconference, which can be set up on virtually a moment's notice. Obviously, as in all other communications to the investing public, it seems rational to release breaking news early—even before market opening (allowing for differing time zones). Negative news is sometimes held until after the market has closed, which may seem to be a clever idea, but which can adversely affect credibility. A University of Chicago analysis suggests that releasing results and having the call after the market closes minimizes the unusual first few minutes of overreaction that sometimes occurs. In view of the increasing amount of after hours trading being done, these classic rules may now be irrelevant, but that, too, is a judgment call.

The conference call at the after-market close has two other advantages—it's backup if the disclosure wires don't print your release, and there are more investors available than when the market is open.

DETERMINE THE TARGET AUDIENCE

Because of the relative simplicity and lower cost in setting up a teleconference, there's more latitude in choosing a target audience, particularly in several cities at once. It can be new or current investors, analysts or brokers. The choice of the group is no different than it is for traditional meetings. For teleconferencing, the minimum useful group is probably about five to eight, although as many as twenty is manageable. More than 25–30 can be unwieldy, especially if questions will be accepted. It may even be feasible to hold several calls, back to back, with different groups with different investment concerns.

For the teleconference, the number is limited only by budget and technical considerations. In view of the original cost of equipment, larger groups are feasible, and for larger companies with larger followings, as many as a hundred people in one video conference is not unusual.

THE INVITATION

A simple e-mail, a one page letter, or a fax on corporate letterhead from the CEO or investor relations professional to investors briefly and directly states the purpose of the call—announcing quarterly results, current update, comment on a known acquisition, comment on a known management change, further explanation of an announced strategic change of direction, and so forth. The invitation shouldn't anticipate the key news, which would take the impact out of the conference, and might not be considered adequate legal disclosure. The notice tells the reader there will be a webcast, internet conversation, telephone or video conference with selected investment professionals or key investors and management, and that there will be the opportunity to ask questions. It should explain who else will be on the call, both management and participants, so that all invitees have a good sense of the company they'll be part of, and can prepare accordingly.

The timing of the letter is a function of both the event and the content. For a conference on news that is closely linked to timely disclosure, the notice should be sent out urgently—perhaps even by overnight courier or fax. For larger events, a week or two beforehand might be appropriate. For internet conferences, e-mail itself becomes the medium for invitation.

As with traditional conferences, some electronic events may require e-mail or phone follow up to invitees.

THE SCRIPT

Preparation—and rehearsal—are necessary for a succinct, focused, and successful conference. Use professional speech trainers, if necessary. Hone the message to specifically address the point of the conference. Anticipate questions, and prepare answers beforehand. Surprises in front of a large group, on a webcast or telephone conference call, can be embarrassing.

Careful preparation is also necessary because interest must be sustained—perhaps even more so than in a traditional presentation. A number of people in different locations are brought together not in a common room, where there is little choice but to focus on the speaker, but at their own desks or computers, where they can be easily distracted. Dull, uninformative conference calls are a profound waste of money. Be interesting, be informative, or you're wasting your money and eroding your credibility.

The techniques and structure of electronic presentations are essentially the same as for traditional meetings. The difference is in the focus of the message, and in the time constraints.

THE EVENT

The more people involved as participants, the more precise the timing must be. The conference should start on time, and end on time.

Even if key people on your staff are not participating, they should be present to supply information and help with questions.

FOLLOW-UP

No contact of any potential value—not an analyst, nor an investor, a broker, a money manager—should be treated as a random participant. Until you have reason to believe otherwise, every contact is a potential investor or someone who will influence investors in your favor.

This means that every conference participant should be added to a mailing list for follow up, and should get, at least . . .

- A thank you e-mail or letter, and an invitation to make further inquiries
- A steady stream of company information at regular intervals
- An invitation to participate in future conferences
- An invitation to ask more questions
- If the individual is sufficiently important, an invitation to come visit, or to meet one-on-one
- An offer of additional sets of material for colleagues and clients

On telephone inquiries following a phone conference, shareholders can be told that if they call an 800 number for the 24-hour period immediately following the completion of the call, they can listen to the entire conference free of charge, possibly including the question and answer session. Shareholders get the first 24 hour period because they have made the financial commitment to the company and deserve it.

Tapes and transcriptions of these programs can be used as mailing pieces to both current and prospective investors. Certainly a transcription can be put on the internet. It can be mailed to media. It can be used as a quarterly report to shareholders. These activities extend the value of the original event.

THE WEB SITE

There is a crucial reality that's too easily ignored in developing a web site. A site is not simply another form of conduit. It's a medium with its own distinctive characteristics. It conveys information in unique ways, and has a different quality of impact. In just a few short years, the web site has become a major tool of corporate communication.

The internet allows a user to log on to your site for a full array of information, from the latest financials to the latest company news to a discussion of management and a list of products. Analysts and other investors routinely check the Web sites of hundreds of companies in which they might invest or that they might recommend, usually as a first step in looking at a company.

The proliferation of authoring programs, such as *Dreamweaver* and *Microsoft Front Page*, and of easy graphic design applications, make producing and getting a site online a relative cinch. Almost anybody can do it, which accounts for the burgeoning of *blogs*—personal web sites that usually contain a consistent core message. It also accounts for a lot of dreary and inept web sites, where professionalism is most demanded. Unfortunately, not every site contributes much more than static and noise for the eye and mind.

The web site of any quality, one that best represents a company, is best designed and managed by a professional. If the site is used for commerce, there are E-commerce specialists.

There are some great sites online. Sites that understand why they are there, and what they are meant to accomplish. What are the differences? What are the pitfalls, and what are the ways to best take advantage of the new medium?

Perhaps the most important difference between a web site and the printed page, and the one that should most affect the site's design, is that a web site is dynamic, and the printed page is not. Information can be changed and updated virtually in real time. The printed page freezes the information until the next printing. The limits of a brochure, an annual report, or other printed material, then, are its size and number of pages. The limits of a web site, including both internal and external links, can be virtually infinite.

Just the ability to link to other pages makes a site a significantly different medium. The printed document may describe a company and its finances, but it's a static description. Pages are generally turned sequentially, like a book. A good web site allows a reader to jump to the information that's most immediate—most valuable—and back again to a home page. This is an extraordinary power in managing and conveying information.

The differences between a web site and other media in the way that messages are conveyed are distinctive and important to realize.

- Just the look of the word or image on a page is different on a computer screen. You can control the look of the printed page, but you can't always control the look of that same information on a computer screen. Different internet browsers show the same images differently.

- The clarity of the image is rarely as good as it is on the printed page. Allowances must be made for these differences in designing a site. Some type faces are more readable than others, for example.
- The use of color is free on the computer. Add color to the printed page and your costs go up dramatically.
- Dynamic motion—images that move—are a major factor on the web site, and obviously, not on the printed page. These devices are relatively easy to put on sites, and if used tastefully, add to the interest and attraction. (But they can also slow down loading time).
- The content, look, design, and colors of a site can be changed at will. Obviously not so in other media. (This is both an opportunity to be creative, and a prospective pitfall that can subvert the message by overwhelming it).
- It's true that many of the elements of a web site can be found in other media. Film and television have color and motion, but at far greater cost. Newspapers change content daily, but a web site can change content in a moment. The amount of text and illustration is limited by the format of other media, but the only limit in a web site is the ability to sustain attention and interest.

These qualities suggest that the site must be designed by someone who really understands the medium, and not just the graphics or content. Designing a web site is a special skill, requiring a greater sense of communication in several dimensions. In fact, it often takes two different professionals, with two different skill sets, to do it right—the communicator, who knows how to get the best out of the medium, and the technician, who knows how to make it happen. A web site, it must be remembered, is ultimately a communications medium—not merely a technical device.

What, then, are some of the major considerations in producing a successful and valuable web site?

- There's an easy tendency to misunderstand objectives. Or more accurately, *expectations*. What do you want the site to do? What can you reasonably expect from it? Name recognition? A display of your firm's skills and capabilities? A demonstration of your firm's breadth and scope? Its growth potential? Your firm's industry and your place in that industry? *What do you want people to know, think, or feel after they've looked at the site?* Without a clear view of objectives for your site, it's impossible to design a site that can accomplish those objectives.

- Given the relative ease with which web site images can be produced, it's easy to allow the design to overwhelm the message. No matter how elaborate the design, including color and graphics, it should let the message do its work. Design should *support* the message and the site, not *dominate* them. Here, artfulness counts. Complex graphics may look great, but may take so long to load that viewers quickly move on to other sites.

- You may have the most attractive site on the internet, but if there's no reason for people to revisit your site frequently, your objectives for it will rarely be achieved. Repetition is impact, as every marketing professional knows. The competition for attention to any one site is overwhelming. Competition for the viewer's attention is fought with a combination of technical skill and artistry (but don't confuse one with the other—they're two different things).

- Think of the difference between sitting straight in a chair in front of a computer screen, and relaxing in an easy chair, reading a brochure. If you want your viewer to get your message onscreen, it has to be easily readable, and worth reading. If you can't sustain interest in large blocks of text, with a message that's interesting and important, then stick to short messages.

- Everybody knows how to read printed text, but not everybody is computer literate. Make sure your site is useable and navigable by the least sophisticated person you want to reach.

- Check your mechanics and links. Make sure your site is accessible to all major browsers (different browsers see code differently) and to major search engines. Keep an eye on loading time. Double check links.

- Today's news gets stale very quickly on a web site. Change content as often as possible. Give the viewers a reason to keep coming back, and to stay on your site for as long as possible. *This is why a firm's web site shouldn't be simply a download of its brochure.*

A good site is an art form, not only in its graphics, but in the professionalism of it ability to convey a message in ways that meet your objective. That's why what makes it so hard is that it's so easy.

EARNINGS PROJECTIONS

In speaking of meetings with analysts and investors, it's impossible not to address the question of earnings projections. Whether spoken or not, and despite the myriad formulae for gauging stock value, earnings projections are very much in the thoughts of every investor—almost as an end product of analysis.

That earnings projections are so integral to judging the investment potential of a stock may be seen in the body of law surrounding them. There is the Safe Harbor legislation of 1995, with its disclaimer and explanation used to ward off litigation arising from a miscalculation or misadventure in projecting earnings. There are the myriad Rules of Disclosure, particularly in the Sarbanes-Oxley Act, that insist that any material information given to one person must, with dispatch, be broadcast to all, which can put a crimp on the value of one-on-one meetings with individual analysts or investors.

An earnings projection by management that can be given any substance or validity is an analyst's dream. It gives the analyst something on which to focus. The assumption is that any well-managed company can make at least a short-term projection of how it's going to perform, give or take a few percentage points, and therefore carries significant weight.

On the other hand, earnings projections have several inherent dangers. They may be viewed as an implied promise of performance that may well preclude factors beyond the company's control. They may place the company's credibility precariously on the line, and are frequently misjudged. A projection of $1.30 that comes out as $1.23 can cause the market to overreact irrationally. A projection of $1.30 that comes out to $1.40 can cause the market to overreact on the upside, or to not react because management apparently doesn't have proper feed-back programs.

An earnings projection also places an additional psychological burden on the management team by causing it to focus its energies on operations toward meeting that projection, which is not management's job.

Of course, properly handled, these concerns can evaporate. For the management willing to come forward and correct previous estimates as new data becomes available, projections can be a no-lose game.

What almost invariably happens, on the other hand, is that the analysts themselves will make a projection in the form of a question. If management chooses not to make a projection of its own, it can simply ratify the analysts' projection as *being in the ball park* or otherwise too high or too low.

Care should be taken that agreeing to an analyst's projection doesn't give management ownership of that projection. If management has decided to make no projection, it should in no way be bullied into it. There are sufficiently sound reasons to explain the refusal to do so if the remainder of the presentation has been forthright.

MEETING WITH INDIVIDUAL INVESTORS

Once an important means of investor contact, new regulation has placed significant strictures on meeting with individual investors and analysts. The inhibiting factor is the extreme danger of inadvertently giving an individual, or a small group of individuals, material information not made immediately known to the public at large under the Rules of Disclosure. The Schering-Plough and Siebel situations, in which extensive fines were levied for violations of Regulation FD, make clear that the SEC takes these infractions seriously.

There are distinct advantages in individual meetings for both the investors and management. The investor usually gets a clearer and more intensive view of management. The questions tend to be more searching and wide-ranging and the executive may be more challenged. Responses are likely to be more detailed than they would be in response to questions from the floor of a larger meeting, And the personal interplay can be helpful to the investor or analyst. And the input from these investors can be valuable.

It's a good idea to keep a record of the meeting—even on tape—so that it can be shown that no inside information was given, should it prove necessary to do so. And again, the Rules of Disclosure must be followed meticulously.

Individual investors, most will find, are extremely accessible, and open to developing a relationship based on their share ownership. Should they hold their stock, or buy more, the investor relations professional's job gets easier.

Individual investors sometimes take, or can be cultivated to take, a very personal attitude toward the company and their investment in it. As such, they can provide some support in difficult times. They also give the investor relations professional a chance to test ideas (within the bounds of SEC rules) and hear directly what end users of investor relations services are thinking. When writing annual reports and interim shareholder reports, it's good to have first hand input about the thinking of some of your audience.

Individual investors hear rumors, which make them good sources for the size and nature of the rumor mill. This can help a company to decide whether to respond, or how to respond, to deleterious rumors, and to stem rumors before they are too widely spread.

In the current configuration of the stock market, the individual investor is emerging again as important, both as an investor and as a source of valuable information. Attention should be paid to them.

MONEY MANAGER MEETINGS

In the realm of important individuals whose needs should be addressed consider portfolio and money managers—the distinctive breed of individuals who manage huge pools of institutional funds, or the funds of high asset individuals. Their potential as prospective investors in any company can be overwhelming, as can be the size of the pools of funds they have to invest. This has been the most fertile area for targeting and segmenting, especially those institutions or capital pools managing more than $100 million.

Their needs for information about a company seem to be more intensive, more urgent. Their tastes and talents, as well as their individual investment theories, put them apart from most analysts. They ask highly technical questions, and demand substantial answers. They want access, and they want performance. They expect you to know about them and what they need before you contact them. As investors, they take large steps.

They are value or growth investors. They are theoretical. There are the *quants* who rely more on numbers than personal factors. There are technicians. There are fundamentalists. Money managers are more interested in macro trends than other investors. The world economy, the U.S. economy, monetary trends and policies, industry trends, momentum trading, new technologies, consumer spending, capital spending, wars, and so forth are all important fodder for them. Yet, like brokers, they are keenly interested in recent market action, in current stock positions—in the same things that concern any investor.

There is no doubt that the more you know about any of these investors the better off you are.

INVESTOR INQUIRIES

Occasionally, a company (and especially those that for one reason or another prefer to remain obscure) will capture the eye of an individual analyst without any effort on the company's part. The analyst then calls the president and asks searching questions. Sometimes an individual investor will feel lonely and concerned and will take it upon himself to call the company president. Nothing inappropriate about it, but sometimes a surprise.

These inquiries should be anticipated by the management of every public company, and prepared for in much the same way as for the presentation for a full-scale analyst meeting. An individual analyst who surprises a company president and gets the wrong answers can do considerable damage to a company's stock, no matter how well the company is doing. There is no need for it. These questions should be anticipated.

All inquiries should be treated courteously and in detail. The company should follow up the inquiry by mailing or e-mailing the same material that it distributes at meetings.

It's extremely important, in anticipating inquiries and preparing the presentation, that the company story be uniformly understood and told by any member of the management team who is likely to get such an inquiry or is designated as a spokesperson. In some cases it's appropriate for the chief executive officer to insist that all such calls be passed on to him or her, to the chief financial officer, or to the investor relations officer. It then behooves the chief executive officer to be sure that everyone who might receive such an inquiry is fully informed of the company's point of view, method of presentation, and proper answers to questions, and the rules of both Safe Harbor and Rules of Disclosure.

FOLLOW-UP

In addition to conducting formalized investor meetings, a properly run investor relations program must include a concerted marketing effort to build and service a following of investment professionals.

Merely to address a meeting of investment professionals does not of itself solve an investor relations problem, or serve as a fully marketing oriented investor relations program. The corporation is, after all, competing against hundreds and thousands of other companies, not only for capital, but for the investors' attention as well. This competition is a continuous effort. Simply because an analyst has met with management and heard its story once, even if that analyst is impressed, there is no reason to believe that interest will be sustained or that the analyst will not be distracted by six other companies that command his or her attention. This interest is sustained by putting every analyst and investment professional who attends a meeting—or expresses any sort of interest—on an active e-mail mailing list. It calls for an aggressive effort to use every appropriate means to sustain relationships with investors.

The analyst must then be contacted periodically, updated on material, reminded of recent information that has been released, and to have any questions answered. It's an ongoing process that, to be effective, must be consistent with marketing principles in both structure and attention.

The mailing list you develop from any source, whether it be individuals who attended meetings or those who e-mailed or phoned with inquiries, or those who responded to any of your efforts, serves a double purpose. It contains the names of prospective investors, and it serves as a prime source for input, feedback and information.

An important consideration in keeping a mailing list is that a company changes, and the investor who was not interested in the company at one point may be interested in it at another. Sound marketing requires assiduous attention to changing needs.

At the same time, you have a marvelous source for learning a great deal about the market for your company's stock. You have the foundation for continuous informal telephone surveys that can arm you with significant competitive intelligence.

For example, a good survey should garner such information as ...

- Whether your major positioning messages are being understood.
- Individual investment goals, and whether they match your positioning
- How many shares they own, how the shares are held, the name of the brokerage house and broker, and when they were bought (also available from corporate transfer sheets)
- How they decided to buy, and how they found out about your company
- What they think about your products, services, and management
- What they think about your recent performance, and strategies
- Are they thinking of adding to their position after calling?
- Did they buy or sell after calling, why or why not?
- Does this program help them to maintain interest in your company?
- Would they be interested in shareholder buying or dividend programs?
- Demographic information, such as income, geographical areas, schooling, product-service usage, age, sex, marital and family questions, etc. For an auto products company, for instance, you might also ask what kind of cars they drive, year, how many, etc.

Over time, these surveys can build a library of important intelligence.

RESEARCH REPORTS

A constant aim, in dealing with analysts, is to generate research reports by brokerage houses or research services. These are reports, issued periodically, for use by both brokers and investors. They may be either brief discussions of the company or intensive, detailed research studies. They almost invariably conclude with a positive, negative or neutral purchase recommendation, or a recommendation to hold or not hold the stock for the longer term. A favorable recommendation by a major research or brokerage firm can be a virtual guarantee of increased buying, and frequently, a higher stock price.

A thorny problem that surfaced during the rash of frauds was the lack of integrity attached to many reports. Analysts for a company's investment banker were issuing favorable, but inaccurate, reports of companies their firms had taken public. Analysts were fudging reports and recommendations for non-neutral purposes. In some cases, relationships with companies for whom the analysts issued reports were tainted.

The SEC, under William Donaldson, and with the help of the Sarbanes-Oxley Act, addressed the problem with a series of regulations that eliminated most of the deleterious relationships, and further regulated the analysts. The objective is to rebuild the integrity the public has a right to expect from the financial community. For the company dealing with analysts, then, there is fair warning that the chicanery and sloth of the past will no longer be tolerated.

At the same time, the practice of paying professional analysts for reports has been surrounded by new regulations that clarify the nature, the authorship, and the provenance of such reports.

A successful investor relations effort includes constantly developing new interest in the financial community for a company. A knowledgeable consultant will be aware, by virtue of consistent efforts in the field, of many analysts and what companies they're following, many of the changes among analysts and their affiliations, and the current basis for viewing companies. The investor relations professional will spend a considerable number of hours every month talking to analysts and other investment professionals to determine those who are likely targets to hear the company's story. Earlier contacts will be followed up to keep them updated and to help maintain their interest. The investor relations professional will develop a constantly expanding following for a company and eliminate those investment professionals no longer interested or no longer available to be interested. This also leads to developing sponsorship for a stock, as well as new market-makers.

In many cases, and only with the permission of the issuing firm, a favorable report may be reprinted and distributed to the shareholders and others in the financial community. Good judgment suggests, however, that an analyst from one firm might be skeptical about a report from another, while some will welcome the input. Don't guess—inquire.

There is, as well, differing legal interpretation of the responsibility that accrues to the company that accepts the estimates in an external analyst's report. Some companies then, refuse to distribute analyst's reports. Others do so with a disclaimer.

FEEDBACK

Feedback of market reaction to the company and its presentation is as much an element of the communication effort as is imparting information. By frequently speaking to investment professionals who follow the company, as well as those who decide not to follow it, the consultant or investor relations officer supplies an extraordinarily valuable view of how Wall Street sees the company. The investor relations professional will identify the problems to be anticipated in telling the company's story, and will be invaluable in determining strategy for meeting objections and for developing sustained interest. The more effective investor relations professionals are those who are fully versed in not only in the techniques of dealing with the Street, but also those whose communication and marketing expertise dovetails with intensive involvement with the largest number of investment professionals and investment companies. This gives them the basis for a constant two-way flow of information and intelligence.

The effective investor relations professional, whether an outside consultant or internal staff, will also supply the company, on a regular basis, with reports of each significant Street contact made in the company's behalf. This includes a report of follow-up discussions with a representative sample of the investment professionals who attended any meeting. The report covers the date of the contact, the person who was contacted and his affiliation and position, what was said by the contact—including negatives—and the consultant's impression of the discussion. This kind of report gives the company an effective and continuous feedback of financial community reaction to both the company and its presentation.

THE BUSINESS PLAN

The interface between a corporation and the financial community, particularly in raising capital, is not always simple to traverse. The language of want and the language of offer are not always the same.

Whether it be for a bank, a venture capitalist, or an investment banker, or if it be for analysts or money mangers who want to better understand a company, the formalized and organized business plan best serves both sides.

Not always simple to prepare, a well written business plan speaks loudly, and gives the best and most accurate picture of a company. The following plan blue print, written for her clients by Lucy Marcus of the international consulting firm, Marcus Venture Consulting *(www.marcusventures.com)* and widely reprinted, is a case in point . . .

Building a Better Business Plan
By Lucy P. Marcus (Copyright © Marcus Venture)

Any business plan is geared to achieve a variety of things, the most important of which is to demonstrate a blueprint for how your company will develop in all of its phases. It is also a document for demonstrating credibility and vision when seeking funding, key employees and strategic partners. However, building a solid business plan that not only snags the attention of key partners, but also acts as the point of reference for a company as it grows, is no easy task.

When looking at business plans, potential investors, employees and partners—and even your early-stage clients—are examining your company to see if it offers an innovative solution. They also want to be convinced the company will succeed in its target market and that the management team offers the breadth and depth of experience to execute on the plan. A good business plan should reflect a company's flexibility to evolve as new models and information come to light, such as changes in the market, in the competitive landscape and in the opportunities that technological developments can afford to your venture.

The proliferation of new businesses, and the growth of entrepreneurship, have given rise to accelerated competition for capital, employees and customers. Every startup competes with a great many other companies for resources and market share. In addition, companies of all sizes must strive to be entrepreneurial in order to succeed in a marketplace becoming more and more competitive every day. This competition begins with the ability to put forth a compelling business strategy. Enter the business plan.

Sum of the Parts

In the end, simply plugging in data is not what makes a good plan. Even if a business plan is well executed, it is often missing a less tangible element—the spirit of the venture and a clear understanding of its goals and objectives. Plans that stand out above the rest are based on a logical progression of concept, supported by the best numbers you can find, solid research, imagination and creativity in approaching your marketplace. Thus, the whole plan should be greater than the sum of its parts.

It is not sufficient to state that your company can capture market and mindshare. It is equally important to prove that your team is the most qualified one to execute on your ideas. More often than not, you might see several plans with a similar business idea—all with potential. In this case, the decisive factor is whether a particular plan approaches the proposed market in a constructive and feasible way, and whether the members of the team are the ones to implement an ambitious and aggressive strategy. This should be the case irrespective of the size of your venture; even if you are a person still operating on your own, you need to have the energy to spark the imagination of others who will contribute to the effort and support your new venture.

Who Should Prepare Your Business Plan?

Your business plan should be the culmination of careful thought and as much expertise as you can gather. If you've never put together a business plan and you are trying to put numbers to ideas, run them by someone who has a clue—don't just put any old numbers in there. If you haven't explored the interesting new possibilities, and even some of the old reliable methods for sales models, find someone who will walk through them with you.

If you are at a developmental phase in your company where you don't have all of this expertise in house, it is important to find people who can help you think this process through, be that an outside consulting firm, a business angel or an experienced entrepreneurial mentor. It is best to find people who have started and run companies before, who understand the reality of what you are trying to create and who have felt the burn of success or failure in being able to achieve these things themselves. On the other hand, this is the plan for your business, and you need to take the ultimate responsibility for it. You shouldn't feel somewhere down the line that the plan put forward is a stranger to you and that you don't really buy into what you are trying to sell—that is a sure way not to succeed.

Build a Plan for Your Company, Not for the Financier

One of the most common mistakes young businesses make is building a plan they believe will ensure that a particular VC will fund them. Going about building a plan in this way is also one of the fastest ways to become frustrated and disenchanted with bringing your business to fruition. In the end, you won't be able to deliver, and you will find over time that there will be an ever-widening gap between goals and results. There are enough funders out there to get a good and sound plan funded—build a plan that will make a good business and it will get funded.

Build a Strong Foundation

Clearly, the minute things start moving—and in aggressive companies these days things are moving fast—the work you put into your plan will pay off. All the thinking, the planning, the exploration and challenges you and your team pursued in the planning stages will pay off as you instinctively move towards bringing it to life. The more carefully you have prepared your plan, the stronger a foundation you will be able to build upon to ensure success when executing your plan.

Dare to Be Different

With the development of technology come new possibilities for sales and distribution. These new methods bring challenges to a budding management team, which must ensure the company is creating a stunning new product or service offering, while at the same time steering a stable and reliable revenue course that will satisfy investors. New distribution methods are perhaps a double-edged sword; they create new opportunities for selling your products, but also put pressure on you to come up with a more complex business plan. Companies today aren't just competing for the best business idea, but also the most unusual sales method.

Building a Dream Team

People are key to your business. A strong and competent team can take a mediocre idea and turn it into a winning business, but a weak and ill-suited team can destroy the best of all businesses. Some important things to think through and address in your plan are: Who are the right people to help you develop and execute your plan? Do you have a plan that will attract—and enable you to keep—the right people? How will you go about attracting them?

Essential Elements: Construction of a Business Plan

Now that you've covered the basic overall themes, it's time to get into the nitty-gritty of writing your business plan. Every person who reads your plan has a checklist in mind. They look for essential information expected in every business plan, so don't hide basic facts. Your business plan will be the closest thing you have to a road map, and it is the thing that will help those around you—funders, advisors and employees alike—understand where you think your business can and will go and how it is going to get there. One thing people often wonder is how long should my plan be? There's no "right" length for a business plan; it should be long enough to give the type of detail that is needed to lay out your plans in a clear and concise way, without wandering down unnecessary paths. That said, a plan over 45 pages long is rarely justified.

I. Executive Summary

The executive summary is your three-minute window of opportunity. It is the place where people decide if they read on to the rest of your plan. It is your opportunity to make a compelling argument for what your company does, to position it within its competitive landscape and to demonstrate why your company will rise above others to challenge what exists and become the leader in its field. Be brief. Two to five pages is ample space to get your point across.

II. Business Description

- An overview of your industry
- A discussion of your company
- Descriptions of your products/services

- Your positioning in the marketplace
- Plans for expansion and globalization

III. The Market

- Market Size and trends
- A clear and forthright outline of your competitive landscape and your position within it
- Current state of the market: competitors, marketshare
- Growth in market and customers and projected movement of your competitors
- Customer base and timeline for growing your customer base
- Estimated Sales

IV. Research and Development

- Development status
- Production process
- Cost of development
- Labor requirements
- Expenses and capital requirements

V. Sales, Marketing and Business Development and Partners

- Marketing strategy and execution
- Marketing communications
- Strategic partnerships
- Sales strategy
- Method of sales
- Pricing strategy
- Sales forecast

VI. Management

- Description
- Ownership
- Board of directors/board of advisors
- Support services
- Plans for organizational expansion

VII. Financials

- Risks
- Revenue projections
- Cash flow statement
- Balance sheet
- Income statement
- Funding request and return

VIII. Appendices

Any supporting materials that further demonstrate the above

Dealing with the Shareholders

They say in marketing that getting the customer is only half the battle. Keeping the customer is the other—and perhaps harder—half. So it is with the company's shareholders.

Keeping shareholders happy is relatively easy in boom times, and not so easy when the market is down and the economy is down and inflation threatens and the jobless rate is threatening. Still, aside from the mandatory information devices, such as the annual report and the annual meeting, there's a great deal that can be done.

The web site has become a primary tool for telling shareholders what's happening. Not just the financial information, but everything else that's going on in the company. The new contracts. The new building. The major new customers. All the good things that happen that make a company thrive.

Shareholders don't like surprises. They don't like being told regularly that things are just great, only to read in the paper or hear on the broadcast media that the company is really in serious trouble. Telling the truth is not only a virtue, it's sound business practice.

In the old days, which was not so long ago, the printed quarterly report carried the company news to shareholders. Today, it's the internet. News about your company is ubiquitous. It's on the broker's sites and on MSN and Yahoo and AOL, and on your own web site. Years ago, informing the shareholder beyond the legal requirements was optional. No longer. The law demands it, but even if it didn't, access to corporate news is so easy that the best reason for your controlling it is to be sure it's told accurately, and to your advantage.

Competing for investors means that if you can't keep your shareholders happy, some other company will.

The Annual Report

For all the communications devices and channels, the traditional annual report is still at the top of the heap. Unlike the internet and the web site, it has heft and staying power. It informs not only the shareholders, but the analysts, the employees, the suppliers, your customers, and the media.

The legal requirements of the annual report are the same as for the Form 10K, and indeed, an increasing number of companies are using wrap reports—an attractive cover with some additional company information wrapped around the Form10K. According to Scott Greenberg, head of Curran & Connors, one of the country's leading producers of annual reports, 10K wraps are overly legalistic, supplying information that any shareholder can glean from the SEC's Edgar web site. Shareholders want more than that, he says, particularly in view of the need for shareholders to be made aware of a company's compliance with Sarbanes-Oxley and the new SEC regulations.

"Under Sarbanes-Oxley," he says, "the company is not legally required to certify a company's financial statements in the annual report, but many are doing so anyway to demonstrate compliance and responsibility."

While the extravaganza reports of the past are not as common as they once were, many companies recognize the value of using the report to go beyond the financials to demonstrate the breadth of the company's activities. They make much of the board of directors, which is a major issue under Sarbanes-Oxley, and frequently supply more industry specific information.

Informal writing, many companies now realize, is better communication. "When a company boasts of 'results-driven value' or 'leveragable knowledge'," says Greenberg, "it's time to take a few steps back before shareholders start scratching their heads in confusion." Writing what your company does in plain English, he says, will convey the message that you're proud of your business.

Shareholders and analysts still believe that, despite the new rulings, annual reports don't say enough. Most companies fail to analyze industry trends, risks, cash flow and capital needs, they say. Accounting policies are not adequately explained, and while many companies are now specifically reporting on non-GAAP financial information, too many are not.

Too little advantage is taken of the Management's Discussion and Analysis ("MD&A") section of the report, including an explanation of its off-balance sheet arrangements in a separately captioned subsection of the report and Form 10K. NIRI's Lou Thompson says that the SEC wants the MD&A to be a principle means of communicating to investors what drives value in the corporation and what management considers the company's prospects for performance. "Warren Buffett put it best," he says, "when he said 'When I read an MD&A, I want to feel like I'm having a conversation with the CEO, who says to me that *these are the issues that concern me most*. I want that level of candor.' "

Ultimately, the annual report is more than a financial report. It's a selling document to the shareholders and all of its other targets.

The Annual Meeting

Of all aspects of shareholder and investor communications, the annual meeting is the one that most CEOs look forward to with measured anxiety. A very serious event in which shareholders have the opportunity to participate, at least vocally, in their company's business, it can also be a time in which questions are asked—some of them quite rudely—and management is challenged. Some shareholders have become known as annual meeting gadflys, going from one to another, vociferously challenging management.

Many meetings have been company events, with souvenirs and favors and free lunch—gala affairs, although in somber days there is less of a party atmosphere and the questions are more serious.

The business part of the meeting is indeed serious. Resolutions regarding company policies are passed, officers and board members are elected, and the CEO gives a state of the company message. When it comes to the resolutions, and the votes, there are all the trappings of corporate democracy, but little of the realities of it. The shareholders are, after all, the nominal owners of the company—rarely with enough shares to make a difference.

Two things are happening that may change that. First, the SEC is plumping to make corporate democracy a reality by introducing mechanisms whereby small shareholders will have the opportunity to put their proposals before the shareholders. Second is the interesting phenomenon whereby institutional investors, with growing awareness of their power as significant holders of a company's stock, are using their votes to affect management policies.

Each year, the legitimate questions from the floor reflect the concerns of the moment. For example, the revolution caused by Sarbanes-Oxley, and the events leading to its passage, will cause concerns about corporate integrity and compliance for several years. In this era of terrorism, safety measures are a concern. Accounting matters are always questioned, as are questions of internal controls and audit committees, and while the days of the trophy CEO are waning, the questions about corporate governance and management compensation are still being raised.

The message is clear, however. The annual meeting is serious business, and calls for management to take it seriously, to be informative, to be presidential, and to demonstrate concern for the shareholders.

The More Things Change

In Wall Street and the financial world, as in the world at large, some things change and some things remain he same. What has changed in recent years is new regulation and new technology, as well as a burgeoning economic environment and globalization.

What has not changed is the competitive nature of the auction market, and the need for the kind of integrity that sustains faith in the reliability of the various and several participants in the market. There is an old saying that the market is always the market. True. But only if the integrity of the market is palpable.

CHAPTER 6

Analysis and Analysts

What Do Analysts Really Want (Besides a Crystal Ball)?

A nalysts, because of their importance to the stock market, stand tall. To the corporation with publicly traded stock, and to the investor relations professional, they are pivotal to successful performance in the market.

And yet, as we saw in the corporate problems arising from the scandals in the first years of the new century, the ground on which analysts stand is not always sturdy.

The litany of their problems is an odyssey that could well have been written by the ancient Greeks. Touting bad stocks as good stocks to serve their firms and their own interests, for example. When WorldCom had filed for bankruptcy in 2002, and its shares were trading for $10.40, Argus Research downgraded the stock to *sell*. A Citigroup analyst, deeply involved with the company and apparently fully conversant with the inner workings of WorldCom, maintained a *buy* or *hold* rating until late June, when the shares had dropped to $1.22. There was a great deal of this kind of thing, and as it surfaced, public skepticism of analyst recommendations blossomed like a weed in a neglected garden. And after an investigation into this kind of conflict of interest, all the major Wall Street firms involved in these practices paid a $1.4 billion settlement.

Then came regulation, which quickly demonstrated the high price of tampering with truth and submerging integrity. Now, analysts must certify that they haven't been paid for the research in their reports and for their public comment. And if they have, they have to disclose the amount of payment, and note that the compensation could influence their decisions.

The ten largest brokerage firms are now required to back up their recommendations with those of independent research firms. The brokerage firms are now required to provide one independent report per stock. Presumably, there is now greater reliability to be found in analyst reports, and—despite the curse of human weakness—greater integrity in the Street.

The real problem, then, is the analytical process itself—the complexity and difficulty of fathoming the value of a stock, and the company behind it—in the light of so many variable factors beyond the control of the company. While extraordinary inroads have been made in understanding the interplay of elements that ultimately dictate market value, the ultimate goal remains elusive. We come close, and continue to better understand how to tame the variables that affect market valuation, but we really have better control in weather forecasting than we do in predicting the future price of a stock.

David A. Hunt and Mark C. Williams, writing in *The McKinsey Quarterly,* suggest that the research arms of the big investment banks are far too expensive given the structural decline in margins in the equities business. They urgently need to deliver more relevant, more original, and better-targeted research. While some analysts have provided company analysis that is useful enough to justify the cost, these individuals remain the exception. They suggest that one way in which the system might work better is by shifting from providing information to insight.

> *While good analysts have always provided original ideas," they say, "far too many researchers have based their jobs on packaging and massaging information. But the appeal to investors of simple information has been limited by the coming of the internet and the passing of Regulation FD, which bars companies from leaking information selectively through analysts. That means undertaking much more in-depth work to generate fresh ideas." Research will now have to include proprietary views on how different industries will evolve and how that will affect each company, they suggest. "An investment bank will have to show how a company is perceived by its customers and to analyze its balance sheet better. Given the expense of this type of fundamental research, investment banks will have to be more selective about the number of companies—and the number of industry subsectors—that their analysts cover.*

In our society, in our economy, the meanings and values of a company are multifarious. A company is, of course, an economic unit. But a company that, for example, creates a hundred jobs in a community in which those jobs had not existed is creating social values. A company that does business using child labor is doing quite the opposite.

But within an economic context, it's not inaccurate to say that the role of a company is to generate economic values, and to provide strategies that generate economic values for its shareholders—its investors. The investor relations professional may or may not have a part in devising those strategies, but the investor relations professional clearly has a major responsibility to define and communicate those strategies.

It would be unrealistic to suggest that investor relations practitioners can unduly influence a stock recommendation if there is no appropriate underlying economic value in that stock. But it's just as unrealistic to expect an analyst or investor to know and understand all of the factors that affect the underlying values in each stock in the market. The role of the investor relations practitioner, then, is to assure that all of the factors about a company are known, understood, and seen in proper configuration and context by those who make or influence investment decisions. It is through clarity of information, not the misinformation of the *spin,* that investors and those who advise them are persuaded.

If the investor relations practitioner, then, is to succeed in transmitting a company's values to this new breed of alchemists, then a great deal must be understood about the analytic process itself, so that the investor relations practitioner may better serve the client company. There are rules. And as in any game, there are skills in playing the game by those rules. But the rules and skills should be known and understood.

Five things make the new analytic environment different...

- The size of the market has increased many times in the past few decades. In the 1970's, for example, a 25 million share day on the New York Stock Exchange was considered a heavy trading day. Today, the average trading day will include more than 1.5 billion shares.
- Scientific methods have been applied to attempt to fathom the mysteries of stock valuation. *Modern Portfolio Theory (MPT),* a sophisticated mathematical approach to delving into the secrets of stock valuation, is now routine. Other refinements and approaches move the science of MPT even further than ever before.
- The computer, with its ability to manipulate and correlate data faster than anything ever before imagined, has made possible even newer approaches, and techniques that couldn't be foreseen a decade ago.

Neural networks, in which data is input so rapidly that it alters the nature of original structure, and then continues to integrate data to the amended structure, on a real time and constant basis, generates an awesome control of relevant information needed to make informed judgments. The art and science of modeling, based on the principles of neural networks and other forms of artificial intelligence, bring a new dimension to analysis. It is as the speed of the horse compared to the speed of the rocket, except that what's traveling so fast is *information*— correlated and integrated data that affects the valuation of a security.

- The internet, with its e-mail, web sites, internet conference calls, brings more information to the analyst and the individual investor alike than was ever dreamed possible a decade ago. Television stations specializing in business reporting now run the tape in real time, which means the tape is now available to anybody with a television set—without the need to sit in the board room of a brokerage firm.

- New regulation, which mandates greater disclosure of more information about a company than had been required in the past. Transparency is of the essence.

This configuration of elements now defines the arena in which investor relations must function.

It's almost impossible to practice effective investor relations without understanding how the analyst works, what kind of information is needed in analysis, and how to be assured that the analyst is not only informed, but understands the information in proper context. Thus, a significant role of investor relations is to supply those elements of information that go beyond the bare facts—to produce a perceived wisdom that tells the prospective investor that this may be the stock to invest in; that this may be the stock that will cause his invested capital to grow.

The raw facts about any public company are readily available—in print, on web sites, through the internet. This is so by law, which requires disclosure by all SEC-regulated reporting companies of specifically defined company activities and performance, results, or information related to past, current and future performance. But if all the most pertinent facts about a company are known and readily available you still wouldn't know enough about the company to invest in it wisely. The investor, or the investment analyst, must still understand considerably more before he or she can make a judgment about the potential success of the company.

According to the Association for Investment Management and Research, the major sources of information the analyst sees as crucial are . . .

- Quarterly and annual audited financial statements—balance sheets, cash flow statements, and income statements
- Footnote disclosures to these financial statements
- Management Discussion and Analysis (MD&A)
- Financial news releases
- Conference calls, site visits, analyst meetings or face-to-face meetings with company management

The analyst's real job is to understand the meaning of the raw data, and how each configuration of data affects the meaning of each of other configurations of data. But that is still just the beginning. Other factors enter into the picture—factors that, as will be seen, are not so receptive to quantification. The investor relations professional's job is to facilitate that understanding.

WORKING WITH ANALYSTS AND PROFESSIONAL INVESTORS

For the investor relations practitioner, working with analysts and investors evolves to two factors—formulating the essence and substance of a company—a position predicated upon reality—and devising the mechanics of communicating both that essence and the substance—the raw data—about the company. But in addition to being a communicator, the good investor relations professional is also an advocate for the company.

It's here that the role of the advocate is really defined. Within the boundaries of ethics and truthfulness, the CEO who understands investor relations, or the investor relations professional who understands the company, moves the facts forward in a forceful and persuasive way. Which is not to say that the facts are moved forward to tell a one-sided story. A story that's all good is too good to believe. Corporate problems, however, do offer opportunities for investor relations professionals to consider the best ways to present the information in ways that, when the analyst or investor makes an assessment, the decision falls your way.

The capital markets are, after all, a competitive arena. The artfulness in presenting the company to the prospective investor resides in the ability to project and communicate the future—those elements that foretell the ultimate success of the company in the market place.

Is that ability artfulness? Probably, in that the difference to the financial community of the stock prices of two companies with the same fundamentals is the degree to which it believes that one company can outperform the other. Because this is frequently a subjective view, the assessment is susceptible to persuasion. Persuasion, within the boundaries of credibility, can be an art.

But it's an art that must be energetically pursued, if a company is to succeed in the marketplace.

And significantly, since it takes two opinions to make a market—one that says the market or a stock are going one way and the other that says they're going another—what are the analytical theories that must be understood if the advocacy role of the investor relations practitioner is to be effective?

THE ANALYST'S VIEW

The analyst is taught to view a company in terms of some rather specific elements, some of which are measurable and some of which are judgmental. Among those factors that enter into the analysis of the company are...

- The financial structure and performance of the company.
- The economic context in which the company operates.
- The nature of the securities market in which the company must be evaluated.
- The nature of the industry in which the company operates, and the market for its products and services.
- The management of the company. Corporate governance has become a major issue. A survey of investors by McKinsey and Company reported that 80 percent of global investors said they would pay a premium for a company that was visibly well governed. But 63 percent said that governance considerations might lead them to avoid certain individual companies.
- The company's own projection of its plan for growth.

According to the Chartered Financial Analysts Federation, the international organization of portfolio managers, securities analysts, investment advisors, and other investment professionals, the key types of information they need are...

- Information about off-balance sheet assets or liabilities
- Explanations of extraordinary, unusual, or non-recurring charges
- Information about pension and other retirement or post-employment benefit plans
- Contingencies, such as litigation or potential exposure to legal action
- Explanations of revenue recognition criteria

They are fully cognizant and wary of the fraud hidden in the off-balance sheet chicanery of the companies that were caught in the financial scandals. CFAF believes that all assets, regardless of how they're financed, as well as liabilities, should be accounted for on the balance sheet, and that GAAP *(Generally Accepted Accounting Principles)* should require it.

Revenue recognition, they point out, is especially critical. Revenue can only be recognized, according to SEC Staff Accounting Bulletin 101, when it is "realized or realizable and earned".

Valuable factors that define the character of the company may include...

- Customer satisfaction
- Product or service quality
- Effectiveness of internal and external information systems
- Marketing prowess
- Market share
- Intellectual capital
- Employee training
- Employee morale
- On time deliveries
- Outsourcings and labor policies
- The changing nature of its industry
- Company integrity, as informed by compliance with Sarbanes-Oxley and SEC regulation

Perhaps the best delineation of the fundamental aspects of security analysis is found in the superb and sustaining work *Security Analysis,* by Benjamin Graham and David L. Dodd (fifth edition, by Sidney Cottle,

Roger F. Murray and Frank E. Block). Benjamin Graham has long been considered to be the dean of analysts, not only for his success as an analyst, but by virtue of the fact that his book was one of the first, and certainly the most masterful, to set forth the basic elements of security analysis. It remains a standard today, and forms the precepts used by successful investors, such as Warren Buffett. Even if Graham's precepts are honored in the breach, they are still a standard that guides all analysts.

Basically, Graham believed that no company should be considered as an investment vehicle unless...

- The company is prominent and conservatively financed. Current assets should be at least two times current liabilities, and debts should be not more than 110% of net current assets.
- The company has been a consistent dividend payer. The more conservative investor would want to see dividends going back twenty years.
- There has been no deficit in the last five years.
- The price-earnings multiple is low. In a soft market, and with high interest rates, he suggests a maximum price of eight times current earnings per share.
- The stock is selling at one half of its previous high.
- The stock is selling at a price that is no more than two thirds of net tangible assets.

Obviously, these are very stringent factors, developed in a different time, in a different market and economic environment. Under many conditions, these principles would eliminate all but the smallest segment of publicly traded companies. And while very little argument can be taken with any of the points he makes, it can certainly be argued that the spectrum of investment possibilities is much greater than companies that fall within his parameters. An example would be a company in an emerging industry with a current ratio of 1.8 but long term debt of 15% of net current assets, and strong earnings gain. Dodd and Graham's credit standards may be too tight for this company, but the company may still be a good investment prospect. During the early years of the high tech companies, it might have been difficult to apply Graham and Dodd's principles, but those principles would have saved a lot of investors had they been followed in the tech industry's later years, before the bubble burst.

The realities of the stock market today, the range of reasons for investments, and new analytical concepts, all dictate some rather more flexible considerations in analyzing a company. In the arena of new companies, with initial public offerings, there are many that, based on fundamentals, are sound investments by any standards.

Another variable today is that with the growing number of investors, new ranges and parameters of risk substantially change security analysis. For example, the value of a stock to an investor with long-term, low-risk goals is different than it is for an investor willing to put investment capital at greater risk to achieve rapid, high returns. Looking at the changing spectrum of risk tolerance, we see new analytical guidelines.

Growing in popularity are new—or newly articulated—concepts of *economic value added* (EVA). It's an attempt to express two concepts—net profit and rate of return—in a single number. A similar program—*market value added*—uses the same approach but with different elements. Whether these programs have any merit will be determined only in the long run.

VARYING ANALYTICAL POINTS OF VIEW

And so, who does the analyzing often determines how it's done. Certainly, the analyst for the bank trust department, functioning in a fiduciary capacity, must be infinitely more conservative than the speculator who is going for high return and who is willing to take a greater risk for it. The analyst for the holdings of 401(k) funds might have very different investment objectives, as dictated by ERISA's Prudent Man Rule, than the analyst for the large sector mutual fund.

The individual investor views a company rather differently than does the fund manager who will be held accountable to others for results. Today's individual investor is somewhat better informed than in the past. The tape watcher who looks to make his profit with every movement of the tape—which can be seen in real time on television or the internet—sees investment possibilities very differently than does the long-term investor who is willing to buy a stock at a very low multiple, but with long-term growth possibilities. The growth of 401(k) pension investment funds have brought in a whole new breed of investors—people who once didn't know a Dow from a Jones, but now watch the tape on cable television and the *Motley Fool* chats on the internet, and the rapidly burgeoning world of mutual funds have moved investment involvement and interest to a larger stage.

The pension fund investment manager, concerned with ERISA's legal concepts of prudence and working within the confines of specific return goals, builds a different portfolio than does the hedge fund manager. All fund managers operate with investment goals, but today, the number of funds and managers has proliferated to a degree that specialization takes on a new meaning. Portfolios are now balanced not just with stocks, but with funds, and funds of funds. One fund will aim at emerging companies, another at mid-capitalization companies, another at blue chips, another at industry sectors or high risk companies, and so forth. This wide array of specialized funds allows portfolios to be fine tuned to meet the specific objectives of each investor. In fact, the growth of the wrap account, in which an investor pays a fee (rather than transaction costs) to a fund manager is made possible only because the fund manager can pick and choose investment funds and investment vehicles to meet the investor's own objectives. What is significant here is that the vast segmentation of the investment community affords opportunity for the investor. For the investor relations practitioner, it means that greater attention must be paid to target audiences, and greater opportunity exists to aim information to the right analytical context.

In this new configuration, analysts in each segment face the problem differently. The analyst for a bank trust department tends to consider investments rather more in terms of preserving capital than does the analyst for the hedge fund, who can invest more aggressively. The analyst for the mutual fund functions in terms of his fund's charter and objectives. The hedge fund analyst is looking for companies that he thinks the market will become enamored with, and whose stock the market would drive up rapidly. The analyst for the growth fund is looking for substantial growth with long-term staying power. The analyst for the pension fund is looking for companies that will not only grow steadily and appreciate over the longer period of time, but have a measure of safety within the fund's definition of needed return. The bank or institutional analyst may have another problem, in that bank and institutional portfolios are often so large that the ability to liquidate in volume is strictly limited. The analysts in the research department of the large retail house must deal with the broader spectrum of companies, because the retail customers have different portfolio needs.

With the magnitude of the market today, retail analysts tend to shy away from smaller public companies, particularly those with less than $200 million in market value. This keeps the analyst's universe more manageable—and certainly more profitable to the parent brokerage firm—because only the largest companies have the volume of shares that can be traded profitably.

REQUIREMENTS OF ANALYSIS

Ultimately, the requirements of analysis of a corporation fall into three categories...

- Financial data
- Management
- Plans

FINANCIAL DATA

Financial data—the financial information about a company—is, of course, the simplest to define. Basic financial data is embodied in the company's audited and non-audited financial statements, its government filings, including its unaudited *Management Discussion and Analysis* of the financial statements, and supplemental schedules. It's made available to shareholders in annual and interim reports, and is readily found on the internet and web sites, and for larger companies, in the business and financial media. The proxy statement also answers some financial questions, and reporting services, such as *Standard and Poor's,* also supply the information.

The SEC has been increasing the depth of financial data it demands in these documents and some companies themselves have volunteered it. Although there are still important areas of operating information that many companies seem reluctant to disclose—quarterly segment reporting is one example—for a public company there is relatively little financial information to which an interested observer cannot become privy. The corporation that tells less deludes itself if it feels that bad news can be hidden from interested parties. More significantly, the reluctant corporation deprives itself of the opportunity to present the company favorably. It leaves itself open to a serious credibility problem, because most analysts feel that if a company is reluctant to disclose and broadcast information of any nature that's relevant to understanding performance, the reasons for doing so must be negative. And since most analysts tend to recoil at the least bit of negative information, any attempt to hide anything causes an almost immediate overreaction.

Remember, too, that the SEC has been absolutely assiduous in its efforts to increase disclosure despite the damage done to disclosure by the courts serving the claimants' lawyers in shareholder litigation, and Sarbanes-Oxley demands it. Overzealous litigation led Congress to pass the Private Securities Litigation Reform Act of 1995, the so-called *Safe Harbor*

Bill, late in 1995, which offers protection against litigation for making appropriately qualified projections that are not met.

Despite attacks on disclosure regulations and policies, or any recalcitrance to full disclosure, one overriding factor remains—the more that is known about a sound company the more readily it will be understood, believed, and favorably viewed.

In analyzing a company's fundamentals, using virtually any process of fundamental analysis, at least the following financial information is essential...

THE EARNINGS RECORD

Since earnings, and the ability to project a company's earnings potential, are a significant aim of most analysis, earnings history is a basic tool. It should be clearly understood, however, that the numbers for earnings never stand alone, and even the traditional view of earnings is constantly being reevaluated. How, for example, can today's earnings, if they're based on non-comparable asset values, be made comparable to the earnings reported two years ago? Thus, earnings are relative to many other factors, all of which must be transmitted to analysts. Certainly, earnings are meaningless except in relation to revenues, as a percentage of revenues. They are meaningless if the role of inflation isn't clear. What is significant in analysis, then, is not just the earnings figure, even when there is a steady increase over the years. It's more important, for example, to note the degree of consistency and growth in earnings and margins. And even this doesn't stand alone, since a growing corporation is affected by many different factors during the course of a year. A sharp growth in earnings may be the result of astute management and a marvelously improved production, distribution, or marketing structure. It may also reflect a merger or acquisition, or a change in accounting practices.

Burton G. Malkiel, the noted Princeton professor and author of *A Random Walk Down Wall Street,* says, "Forecasting future earnings is the security analysts' raison d'etre. Expectations of future earnings is still the most important single factor affecting stock prices." Growth (in earnings and therefore in the ability to pay dividends or to engage in stock buybacks) is the key element needed to estimate a stock's firm foundation of value, he points out.

"The analyst who can make accurate forecasts of the future will be richly rewarded. If he is wrong, a stock can act precipitously, as has been demonstrated time and time again. Earnings are the name of the game and always will be," says Malkiel. Analysts, he says, generally start by looking at past wanderings. It is assumed, he points out, that a proven score of past performance in earnings growth is a most reliable indicator of future earnings growth. If management is really skillful, there is no reason to think it will lose its Midas touch in the future. If the same adroit management team remains at the helm, the course of future earnings growth should continue as it has in the past, or, he says, so the argument goes. Such thinking flunks in the academic world. Calculations of past earnings growth are no help in predicting future growth. If you had known the growth rates of all companies during, say, the 1980–90 period, this would not have helped you at all in predicting what growth they would achieve in the 1990–2000 period.

"There is no reliable pattern," he says, "that can be discerned from past records to aid the analyst in predicting future growth. Bluntly stated, the careful estimates of security analysts (based on industry studies, plant visits, etc.) do little better than those that would be obtained by simple extrapolation of past trends, which we have already seen are no help at all. Indeed, when compared with actual earnings growth rates, the five-year estimates of security analysts were actually worse than the predictions from several naive forecasting models.

In the final analysis, he says, financial forecasting appears to be a science that makes astrology look respectable. "When one considers the low reliability of so many kinds of judgments, it does not seem too surprising that security analysts, with their particularly difficult forecasting job, should be no exception," says Malkiel. "There are, I believe, four factors that help explain why security analysts have such difficulty in predicting the future. These are (1) the influence of random events, (2) the creation of dubious reported earnings through creative accounting procedures, (3) the basic incompetence of many of the analysts themselves, and (4) the loss of the best analysts to the sales desk or to portfolio management."

Malkiel is right. The *quality of earnings*, an analysis of earnings predicated upon factors that are not immediately discernible, such as accounting changes that can alter the measure of earnings in ways that don't accurately reflect the company's actual performance, means more than the numbers themselves. Historical earnings in the pure sense are themselves of limited value in gauging the ability of a company to continue to earn at a consistent rate.

With inflation or the broad fluctuation of raw material costs, the historical cost, for example, of raw material or finished products in inventory moves a great distance from current or replacement cost. How, then, can assets be valued on a comparable historic basis? How can today's earnings, if they're based on inflated costs and prices, be made comparable to the earnings reported two years ago? In fact, how can earnings comparisons be made unless there is a comparable basis for accounting for added risk taken on by the corporation to produce continued gains? The fact is that without some significant changes in accounting practices, they can't be made comparable.

While analytical methods that emphasize earnings growth have been important in recent years, and are still the most widely used, their shortcomings have become increasingly clear. The complexity alone of some methods almost automatically produce controversy. For example, the prestigious Boston Consulting Group offers a formula to define sustainable growth as a measure of created value. Alfred Rappaport, in his excellent book, *Creating Shareholder Value* (The Free Press, NY 1986), labels the formula "an unreliable indicator of value creation."

Properly analyzed, however, the factors behind a consistent earnings history are a measure of elements that contribute to ongoing earnings growth, and are usually a good indicator of a company's success. The key is to expand the concept of the factors behind, and in addition to, earnings. And successful investor relations depends upon the ability to impart to analysts not only the dynamics of earnings, but those other factors that enhance the value of the company's securities

REVENUES

Revenues (not to be confused with *sales*) are often used as a measure of the size of a company—a way of categorizing the economic sphere in which it functions. Revenues come from many sources—sales of products or services, investments, sales of assets, and so forth. Obviously, it may be readily inferred that many factors about a company with $500 million in revenues are different from those of a $25 million company. The large company is more likely to be older and better established, except in certain emerging industries such as computers and communication technology, where growth has been explosive, and would seem to have an even greater potential for growth and survival. It probably has a better grasp of its markets. It probably has a larger number of shares outstanding and a greater market value and liquidity in the stock market. It probably has a greater ability to withstand broader economic difficulties. Yet it mustn't be taken for granted that a very large company has any greater ability to succeed, or for its growth to compound faster, than does a smaller one. The number of giants that have fallen on hard times in recent years is too large to take size alone as a measure of investment safety. Witness AT&T and Kmart, for example. IBM declined sharply, until it got a new CEO, and then rose again. Apple Computer was down, until new products, like the IPod, saved the day. There are, in fact, fairly reliable measures of growth. Rappaport, in *Creating Shareholder Value*, discusses techniques for measuring *fundable rate of growth* and *affordable sales growth*. He warns that growth rate should be an outgrowth of strategy, and not the other way around.

CASH FLOW

Because of some of the problems associated with earnings-based analytical formulas, more analysts are turn to cash flow analysis, which they believe gives a truer picture of how a business is being run. Cash flow, many analysts feel, levels all the accounting acrobatics that sometimes obfuscate the picture of a company. The concept is an old one in economics that says that the value of an investment is derived from its cash flow—the organization's basic cash-in, cash-out.

Basic cash flow is most simply defined as net income plus depreciation. But, depending upon their needs and personal concepts, many investors use other definitions and measures. For example, one group of investors prefers to look for *operating cash flow*, which is the money generated by the company before the cost of financing and taxes. According to analysts at one investment firm, *Goldman, Sachs & Co.*, a portfolio of stocks with the best *price to operating cash flow* ratio would, in 1988 and part of 1989, have doubled the return of the Standard & Poor's 500 stock index.

Today, an increasing number of analysts and investors look to current and prospective cash flow before they analyze other factors. They believe that *discounted cash flow*—estimated future cash flows discounted back to present value—has more potential for judging company and stock market success than earnings-based analyses. Cash flows are discounted by the cost of capital or an average of debt and equity.

Probably the best of these kinds of measures is *free cash flow*, which is earnings plus non-cash charges, less the capital investment needed to maintain the business (there are other definitions). It's a measure of discretionary funds—money that can be taken from the company without jeopardizing it.

Holt Value Associates, one of the leading security analysis services, introduced its *Value Focus* service, based on economic cash flow return on investment (CFROI) performance, and not reported accounting information. This is an example of the increasing acceptance of cash flow-based concepts today.

MARGINS

Normally, *net margin*—the percentage of net income to revenues—is relatively simple to measure. It's a major factor in determining both the efficiency of a company and its ability to cope with costs and expenses—both of which constantly change. Margins are affected by increasing competition in an industry in which product pricing becomes a significant competitive factor. Margins become even more significant in a period of unstable prices or raging inflation, when gross margins might reflect vast swings in the cost of raw material and labor. Under those conditions, the margins can be severely hit if the company is not able to pass on to its own customers the high cost of any basic materials. Margins affect the quality of earnings, when many companies must sell from inventories that had been built up at lower costs, and were reported at inflated prices. In many cases, this results in a distorted picture of the company's realistic margin, since it's difficult to discern the consistent level of future costs for the same items. When this happened in the past, many companies changed their method of depreciation to reflect accelerated deflation. Today, that inflationary factor is built into many corporations' financial structures, further distorting margins as well as earnings. Too, the computer's ability to recalculate on a real time basis keeps the report of margins current, usually enabling adjustments without broad swings in pricing.

RETURN ON EQUITY

This is the *earnings per share divided by the book value (the difference between a company's assets and its liabilities)*. Return on average equity gives a more accurate picture than return on beginning equity because it accounts for the equity added during the year and, therefore, presents a more complete picture. Many companies now use average equity in its calculations. For investors, this is a most significant measure of a company's success. It is, after all, what investment is all about. If the return on any investment in one company isn't as high as it is in another—and assuming that the difference isn't offset by dividend yield, or that the achieving company isn't so highly leveraged that it's threatened by high interest rates—then what's the point in investing in the company with the low return?

BALANCE SHEET

The balance sheet still offers the best picture of a company's financial position—as of the date of the balance sheet. If the balance sheet of *Enron,* had been heeded, then its favorable earnings reports issued immediately prior to its bankruptcy might have been viewed with a bit more skepticism. The balance sheet does—or should—tell the analyst a great many things. It also poses a great many questions. And it behooves the corporation to anticipate these questions in order to prevent misunderstanding or misinterpretations, as well as to clarify the position of the company. There may very well be justification for a very high inventory or a substantial increase in inventory from one year to the next. For example, a major customer under a multi-year contract may have deferred deliveries from the fourth quarter to the first quarter of the following year. The balance sheet alone will merely indicate the size of the inventory. It will not explain it. A reduction of cash from the prior year against a reduction of debt implies that the cash was used to reduce the debt. Without explanation it is merely an implication. Certainly a disparity from one year to the next in accounts receivable or accounts payable warrants an explanation, even if it's an unfavorable one. The growth of pension fund assets poses an increasing balance sheet problem particularly under current accounting treatment, because the unfunded pension liability portion can be larger than it should be—a great worry to investors.

While the notes to financial statements usually clarify the debt structure, questions about debt—both long and short term—go beyond the balance sheet. The balance sheet, it must be remembered, is as of a particular date. Debt can be increased or decreased the day after the closing of a balance sheet, as can any element of the assets or liabilities. This is a prime example of why a balance sheet never speaks for itself in describing a company; the analyst wants to know more that it can show. And with accounting standards rapidly changing, the company must be prepared to defend its accounting methods.

The real time aspects of the internet may help by allowing for a running balance sheet, with changes reported as they occur. But for comparison, the dates must be consistent.

RATIOS

The analysts, with their computers or electronic calculators, can compute a head-spinning number of ratios, many of which, like astrological symbols, can assume meanings of varying importance for different people. Ratios without explanation frequently imply a picture that, in view of changing conditions and other factors, may not be accurate in terms of the corporation's actual operations. Ratios, like any statistics, are a still picture of a corporation frozen at the moment the picture was taken, while the corporation continues to move on. It's extremely important that any ratio that differs from the industry norm, either up or down, is a signal for the need for elucidation and explanation.

The array of ratios is imposing. The ratio of *current assets to current liabilities,* if it is less than two to one, sends a red flag flying. If the *debt to equity* ratio is too high, the analyst immediately wonders about the drain on future earnings by debt payments. The ratio of *return on total capital.* The ratio of *depreciation and depletion to sales.* The ratio of *earnings paid out in dividends to earnings.* The *price to sales ratio* for smaller, high technology companies. And this is exclusive of ratios of various factors such as earnings, dividends, assets, and sales to the market price of the stock. Graham, in his book, *Security Analysis,* leans very heavily on ratios as a measure of company performance.

Theodore H. Pincus, retired chairman of the investor relations consulting firm, The Financial Relations Board and an investor relations pioneer, believes that the ratio of the *price–earnings ratio to the company's average growth rate* over a specified period-the *PEG* ratio—is very useful to analysts. An average growth rate of 15 percent during the period studied, and a P/E ratio of 30, would give a company a *PEG* ratio of 2-to-1. Using *PEG* ratios for various companies, analysts can get a good sense of whether a stock is too high or attractively low. This is not the same, however, as the old adage about buying a stock selling for one-half its growth rate, and is infinitely more useful.

COST OF CAPITAL

Some aspects of the cost of capital, such as the prime rate inflation, and taxes, are fairly evident. The company that must function heavily with short-term borrowing, such as a leasing company or an importer who depends upon revolving credit lines, will find itself in serious trouble when the prime rate starts to climb. The company that is fairly heavily leveraged—has a very high debt in proportion to its equity—is also in serious trouble. The expansion-minded company is always viewed in terms of its financial ability to expand either internally or externally. Even in an atmosphere that allows for additional capital through equity, the analyst must consider the cost of a company's equity capital in terms of its price/earnings ratio. This whole area then becomes a matter of major concern for analysts, and therefore of major concern for the corporation that wants to explain itself.

Increasingly, cost of capital and Capital Asset Pricing Models (CAPM) have become a focus of attention of analysts. In his publication, *Valuation Issues*, William F. Mahoney writes, "Corporate managements are focusing more on lowering their company's cost of capital, recognizing its importance to investors seeking to maximize returns of their portfolios." The goal, he says, is to achieve returns above the cost of capital. There is a great deal of controversy surrounding CAPM as a valid measure of risk, but the models serve as a valuable tool for company financial officers in measuring company performance, and are therefore a valuable element to communicate to analysts.

In *Creating Shareholder Value*, Rappaport clearly explains that the cost of capital is a crucial factor in deciding whether shareholder value—the worth of the company—is being enhanced. He lists formulas to determine whether a company earns or will earn a return more than its cost of capital. If so, shareholder value is created. If not, no value may be created, or a company's value might actually go down.

A somewhat similar method of analysis is *Market Value Added* or *MVA*. This is the cash investors put into the business over its lifetime, measured against the amount they could get out by selling their stock today. Then there's *EVA—economic value added,* which is net operating profit after tax, minus the weighted average cost of capital. Every analyst, it seems, has a preference among ratios. Some may be right. All must be served by the investor relations professional.

THE INDUSTRY

Each industry has distinctive characteristics and requires analyzing additional elements, with a different emphasis on common elements. Sources and uses of funds and revenues differ. Accounting methods differ. Industry practices differ. Nevertheless the same rules of communication apply. All of these differing characteristics must be clarified to investors and analysts. Because the same ratios mean different things in different industries, ratios and changes require explanation, and nothing should be taken for granted.

For a company to represent its financial situation as independent of the industry in which it functions, or even of the larger economy, is to delude itself. Even the company that's out-performing its industry for one reason or another must still realize that in most cases it's being judged in terms of its industry. No company president functions successfully without intensive knowledge of his industry. But too often companies are presented to analysts without a clear explanation of comparable performances, common and uncommon problems and solutions, distinguishing industry characteristics, costs of raw materials and distribution, potential markets, and so forth.

CHALLENGES OF INDUSTRY SPECIALIZATION

There is yet another challenge in that analyzing specific industry groups usually falls on a small segment of analysts who specialize in that industry. This poses two serious concerns. First, a company judged by industry specialists, no matter how well it is performing, is often given the same general value by the market as is the industry itself. If the industry is depressed, even a superior company within that industry can face serious stock market problems.

Second, the majority of analysts who fully understand the ramifications of a particular industry rarely change the relative rankings of major companies within that industry. If you are seen as number three in the industry, you are usually the number three forever, with that P/E seen as the norm for your company, unless there is a major company event or breakthrough of some kind. Moreover, most of these industry analysts don't always represent a sufficiently large number to warrant devoting a major portion of an investor relations effort to them. It therefore becomes necessary to deal with a larger group of analysts functioning in other contexts, and in other organizations, who are not as well versed in the ramifications of a particular industry as are the industry specialists, but who may nevertheless see other values. The communications effort then becomes more challenging. Not only must the company be explained and sold to analysts, but the complex specialized differences in dealing with the industry and the company and analyzing it must be made clear.

The problem of specialization also arises frequently in dealing with companies with large international operations. Even in today's international environment, where more companies than ever before have some degree of international activity, there are still a relatively small number of American analysts who feel they have the broader international economic background to properly assess a company with significant international activity. Too many others tend to ignore such companies and move on to those easier to understand. There are, after all, more companies in the broader economic sphere than any one analyst can follow. At the same time, there are analysts who specialize in dealing with only one or two companies, particularly if those companies are large enough to represent a major factor in the international economic scene.

These are the significant financial factors that must be communicated in judging a company. It should be clear, however, that in dealing with analysts and others who judge companies, numbers shouldn't be presumed to speak for themselves. They never do. They require elucidation and explanation. This is why financial statements have footnotes. It can't be repeated too often—a corporation's statistics freeze the picture as of the date of those statistics, and corporations are dynamic entities.

Prognostication for an entire industry is somewhat easier, at least within a limited range of time, than it is for any one company within that industry. The economic indicators of an industry are rather simple to define. If consumer spending is down as a result of economic recession, for example, or the economy is in a period of high consumer debt such as existed in late 1995 and into 1996, it's reasonable to assume that retail purchases in certain industries, such as appliances and apparel, will have trouble achieving earnings records. Competitive factors, such as online and catalog sales, adversely affected retail chains. If there are basic material shortages, with no relief in sight, it's reasonable to assume that those industries using those materials will have problems. In good economic times, the purchasing power increases, but selling labor gets scarcer.

When transistors were invented, transistor manufacturers enjoyed a boom in those products that used transistors, such as miniature portable radios and portable tape recorders. But then as the industry became saturated with transistor manufacturers, and technology reduced the cost of transistors, it became impossible for any company to compete successfully and with very high margins, and the transistor stocks fell on their faces. New technology helps, but is volatile. The advent of the Pentium chip caused Intel to soar—until Cyrix came up with a cheaper chip. Technology, analysts know, is a two-edged sword.

On the other hand, when a new industry emerges, such as computers, there are a new set of problems and opportunities. At first, there was a shortage of analysts and investors who fully understood the nature of the industry and where it might go. Then, as it began to grow and mature in the United States, new competitive forces came into play. No sooner did analysts and investors begin to grasp the basics of the new industry when both new technology and competition changed the scene. In the beginning, computer stocks, such as *Compaq* and *Lotus,* were at first undervalued, and then, as the companies broke growth records, moved into new competitive contexts that few analysts really understood. By the time the industry had matured, shares of market had shifted, markets became saturated, new technology changed and challenged leading companies, and there were new economic configurations that were unfamiliar to most investors. By the time the financial community began to understand *Compaq,* it was a mature company, revaluated its market, and redesigned its product line and marketing approach. By the time the financial community began to understand the pioneer Lotus, the company ran into marketing problems, and wound up being acquired by *IBM. IBM,* which had been overwhelmed by *Dell* and *Compaq (now H-P),* and dropped from its leadership position, began it's own comeback. At the same time, small companies get very big very fast—look at the giant *Microsoft*—and big names and former high fliers, like *WordPerfect,* virtually disappeared. Now, with the burgeoning of the internet, and the growth of communications technology (e.g. the cellular phone), things continue to change. As the popular industry writer, John C. Dvorak, puts it, "everything you learned this week will be obsolete by this time next week." This is how a new industry affects the financial community, in which technology moves faster than analysts can fully understand its nuances and ramifications.

Industry analysis is not without problems for the investor relations professional. Analysts tend to minimize, for example, the company that is outperforming its peers. They frequently fail to understand longer term industry trends, or the effects of new technology on the performance of a company, nor do they readily accept turnaround situations early in the turnaround performance. Despite all the warning signs, in 1981 analysts still expected $100 oil in the energy industry. *IBM,* not long ago, was considered dead. Mini-mills saved a part of the steel industry. Perspective seems to be a foreign word to the finance industry.

Sometimes industry analysts find themselves susceptible to the same kind of short-term response to which the individual investor is victim. One of the groups to be hit when it was first announced that the plastic, polyvinyl chloride (PVC), was a factor in producing cancer in both the PVC industrial worker and the consumer was the plastics industry. Plastics analysts felt that most plastics manufacturers would be subject to regulation that would either curtail production or involve large capital investment in safety equipment. It took a considerable amount of time, during which plastic stocks were adversely affected, for the analysts to sort out those companies that were unaffected, or had already built safety factors into their production.

The problem of environmental pollution lends itself to a similar potential for overreaction. Many industries—paper, steel, chemical, utilities—are now subject to production strictures that will affect their processes, and attendant costs, to varying degrees. But there are relatively few facts available on how these strictures are to be defined or how to judge the costs for individual companies, much less specific industries, particularly with uncertainties as to the future of environmental regulation under current and future administrations. Very little research has been done in this area, and without facts, overreaction is found to be the rule.

In the arcane world of economic influences upon company analysis, the burden is on management—and by extension, the investor relations practitioner—to clarify, to explain, to define context. For example, when the price of the dollar on world markets changed abruptly a few years ago, it made it seem that companies with large overseas operations were losing revenues and profits. But given an understanding of foreign currency translations, those companies with better investor relations communications and marketing skills fared better in the stock market than did other companies in the same plight. More recently, when the dollar was falling against the Euro, U.S. companies raced to do more business overseas and that message has helped the stocks of *Coke, McDonald's, Caterpillar* and others perform better in the stock market.

ANALYZING ECONOMIC CONDITIONS

In a growing economy, such as we enjoyed for an extended period of time in the 1990s, even stranger things happen in the stock market than during a period of no growth or economic uncertainty. Bad times seem to make investors depressed, but good times seem to make them nervous. How else to explain that in the longest period of sustained growth in generations, every time there's good economic news, the market drops substantially?

The recovery from the recession following the tech stock failures had its own unique qualities, in which increased productivity, driven by sophisticated computers, didn't include an increase in jobs. The effect was unique in the economic history of the country.

One common explanation for the caution of American industry is that the history of double digit inflation is too fresh in people's minds. Good times mean inflation. Inflation is controlled by the Federal Reserve Bank's raising interest rates. Raising interest rates affects both the bond market and interest sensitive stocks.

And obviously, economic events affect the market.

Changes in health care law affect the insurance and health care industries, which affects the economy. The growth of HMOs has substantially altered the economics of health care, affecting not only the health care stocks, but the financial performance of all industries and all companies in which health benefits are a large portion of operating expenses.

In a sense, the economy is like an ecological structure, in which no event is isolated; every event affects all other tenets of the system, and does it with different timing in different segments of the economy. No economic leaf falls without affecting the entire environment.

Analyzing economic conditions is an arduous and sometimes frustrating task, and rarely do two economists agree on the meaning of any one event. But unless the company itself supplies the guidelines for evaluating the effect of these external economic factors on its own performance, the judgment by analysts as events unfold will almost invariably be an overreaction or underreaction. The responsibility for putting any economic news in perspective, even before its effect is felt by the company, resides with the management.

For all its apparent sophistication, economics is a most inexact science. Just when everybody thinks the arcane science has been tamed, some new and unforeseen element enters into it. A war. Currency devaluations. Inflation. Political uncertainty, such as the change from a Democrat to Republican-controlled Congress. A savings and loan crisis. A decision by the Federal Reserve Bank to tighten up the money supply. A drought. A bankruptcy by a major company. And on and on and on.

Everyone knows where the economy has been and sometimes people even know where the economy is. But nobody ever really knows where it's going, despite computer models, economic indicators, or the ability to read the future in the entrails of sheep. Obviously, this throws even the best analysis into a cocked hat. It moves it out of the realm of the economic certainty of a balance sheet, and the historical value of the earnings records, into a vast world of major uncertainty. It's not without its charm, however, in that it offers analysis the excitement of prognostication that one rarely gets with just the electronic calculator or even the computer.

PROJECTING MANAGEMENT CAPABILITY

The two most important intangible factors of a company that must be judged by analysts are its management and its plans. There are in American industry today many large companies that began as small companies. There are also many small companies—and many that no longer exist—that were started at the same time as companies that are currently large. One difference between two companies that started small, and of which only one thrived, is capitalization. The other and major difference is management, which, given management's role in raising capital, may in some measure be the same thing.

A study by the University of Iceland found that about 40% of the difference in the herring catch among the 200-boat fleet depended upon the captain. A look at hundreds of top companies in the U.S. and Canada showed that the personality of the CEO made as much as a 15% to 25% difference in profitability.

Management is less exact a science than long-range weather forecasting, and probably more arcane, mercurial, and convoluted. Judging management talent and skills can be difficult, not only because they're intangible, but because they're highly subjective. The elements of management may be definable, and with computer modeling, the science of divining those elements is undoubtedly improving. What is *not* definable is the way the configuration of those elements will function in terms of results. And as business grows in intricacy, so too do the demands on management become more complex, and so too does analyzing and assessing management become more speculative. Ultimately, and despite what they say in business schools and books, successful management is a function of skill, talent, personality, and luck.

Part of the problem of fathoming management, most analysts are finding, is that successful management can no longer be judged by traditional standards. The world moves more quickly than ever before, and using traditional methods of judging the skills of management is much like comparing the techniques of flying a single-engine prop plane to flying a jet in combat. The old skills are no longer any good in a world in which competition is international, the sources of capital are multifarious, technology changes the environment radically on a moment's notice, and the skills needed to run a company and to compete successfully include those that didn't exist a decade ago. And all this must be communicated to people who must make investment decisions based on information that travels with the speed of light. Success in investor relations, then, becomes more than a simple communications function—it becomes an art form.

The broad definition of management is the subject of a full library of theories, many of which conflict and none of which is definitive. What is important in investor relations is the ability to project to investors, believably, a corporate management's ability to manage its company, to cause it to thrive and to grow, and to survive, in both good and bad times. What's crucial to project is management's ability to create shareholder value.

Management theories abound, and continue to proliferate. But for the most part, complex management theories obfuscate, rather than help, security analysis. Essentially, the different theories are simply different routes to the same goal—increasing shareholder values. Whether the company is run from the top down, in the traditional model, or by a creative team, which seems to be the model in many high tech companies that require vast input from many people, the goal is still the same. And so too is the need to judge management's ability to meet that goal.

A person who invents a cure for the common cold may be a thoroughly bad manager in terms of marketing, production, or finance. The entrepreneur who invents a useful and valuable item in his garage may be capable of managing the company he develops with his invention until sales reach a level of $30 million a year. As his or her company continues to grow, the shape of the company alters, production needs change, and so, then, do administrative needs. Team strength should be developing. A company in transition is at its most vulnerable point. The entrepreneur who is capable of building it to $50 million may not have the capabilities to build it to $100 million. The management team of a one-product company that decides to expand its product line or to diversify suddenly faces new and generally unfamiliar problems and may not be able to cope. Again, team strength emerges, as a topic increasing in importance.

A good management team must have a grasp of a great many things—finance, marketing, administration, production, distribution, the economy in general and its industry in particular. And even within the context of these elements, abilities are limited and alter with changing conditions. And again, never underestimate the value of personality and luck.

Perception, in looking at a company, is often very different from reality. The problem is that too often, the facts don't count—it's what people perceive to be the facts on which they make judgments. This puts a particular burden on the company, and a profound responsibility on the investor relations practitioner.

In projecting management capability, three views must be defined...

- The chief executive officer's talents, personal characteristics and leadership
- The capabilities of each key member of the management group
- The team of managers itself... its interaction and effectiveness as a team

THE CEO AS LEADER

Obviously, the chief executive officer, at the helm of the corporate vessel, is crucial to the success or failure of the enterprise and it's voyage. Aided by the management team, guided, presumably, by the board of directors, the CEO has the key responsibility for vision of the firm, and for translating that vision into a reality that enhances return on investment. The CEO, while not necessarily capable of bringing full expertise and experience to every task in a company, must at least have a solid understanding of the full range of management skills, from marketing to finance to production and distribution. He or she must lead the planning and execution of the corporate operation, motivating others who must make the vision a reality. The concept of risk is always operative in the executive suite—risks to new markets, risks to new products or services, risks to capital expenditures, and the toughest risk of all—the risk of doing nothing. The successful CEO can see around corners, be able to turn the ship on a dime, repair it if it breaks down, and get all hands pulling in the same direction.

It is this capability that must be projected to prospective investors and analysts.

It's significant to note that, at the turn of the century, we passed through a phase that contributed to not just the scandals of the time, but the peculiar turns taken by corporate America—the charismatic CEO. The CEO as not just a corporate leader, but as a personality. As it turned out, some were good for their companies—the larger than life GE chief, Jack

Welsh. Some were so riven by hubris that they were indicted—Dennis Koslowski of Tyco. Some were heads of companies completely intertwined with their companies, and very successful at it, such as Martha Stewart. Her problems arose from personal choices, not from company mismanagement. Some, like Microsoft's Bill Gates, were lionized solely for their management skills, and not for their personalities. This was the cult of the charismatic CEO.

At the same time, it began to become clear that most of the successful CEOs were not part of that cult. They were simply quiet and humble men and women who did their jobs, and served their companies and their employees and their shareholders without fuss or fanfare—simply by running their companies well and successfully.

The mercurial personal qualities necessary for successful leadership are difficult to define, and the elements of success have long been the fixation of major articles in leading business magazines, books, and the academic world. What personal qualities might be successful? Brains, hard work, a talent for delegation, for choosing the right team members, a flair for marketing or production, creativity, honesty, articulateness, education, experience, charisma? What makes Gates and Allen and Welch tick? Is there some formula—some *seven habits*—that can be distilled and transmitted to CEOs of lesser talents?

Chief executive officers have been getting more scrutiny than ever before. Not all this attention is welcomed, particularly when it questions executive compensation, or an unusual acquisition or divestiture, or any other high risk decision, or personal life styles that impinge upon corporate activity. The CEO is always in a precarious position, and the degree to which he or she is willing to take risks, or manage risks, is an important measure of CEO effectiveness. As with today's top athletes and movie stars, large amounts of increasing remuneration beyond what the average investor makes brings increased public responsibilities. These large sums are being granted to senior officers, causing a measure of consternation among shareholders who earn considerably less. In fact, it could be argued that compensation is, in part, for the risk as well as the performance.

The scandals of the early years of the 21st century place a burden on the modern CEO to demonstrate that his or her company—the number of CEOs who are women is increasing—is run for the success of the company and its shareholders, and not just the personal reputation of the CEO. This redounds to the benefit of shareholders. It's a tool in the arsenal of the investor relations professional. Sarbanes-Oxley may mandate behavior that keeps the CEO's nose to the grindstone. It's the investor relations professional's job to see that the investment community understands not just the CEO's abilities, but his or her integrity as well. After the scandals, trustworthiness is currency in the marketplace.

In the final analysis, the best guide to a company's potential for increasing shareholder value is the measure of the man or woman at the head of the firm. Projecting the elements that clarify and define those qualities is at the heart of successful investor relations.

THE SENIOR MANAGERS

While the company's vision emanates from the CEO, the job of making that reality a vision begins with the senior managers—and analysts and investors know it.

Analysts want to understand the talents of the key managers and even directors. What do they add to or take away from the management team? Who are they, what do they know, what do they contribute, and where do they come from?

Which of them is capable beyond his or her assignments? Who's next in line—the finance officer or the marketing director?

Which of them seems to work well with the CEO and which does not? Is there harmony or friction?

For the astute analyst, the answers to these questions are as significant as understanding the personality and skills of the CEO, and this should be a guide to the investor relations professional's communications plan.

THE MANAGEMENT TEAM

A good management team must have, as a group, a grasp of a great many disciplines—finance, marketing, administration, production, distribution, the economy in general and its industry in particular. And even within the context of these elements, abilities are limited and alter with changing conditions. How the team works together—its members' ability to cooperate with and support one another, their chemistry together—is significant information for analysts. It's a crucial measure of the potential success of a company.

When economic conditions are good and sales are coming easily, and the company is adequately financed and there are no production problems, a management team can be perfectly capable of showing profits. But how can an analyst judge how that same management will function when money becomes tight, when competitors start hitting the market, when a strike hits the plant, when there is a material shortage, when there is a takeover attempt by another company, when there are price controls, or when—as in the case of the transistor problem—the market becomes saturated with its product? Every management team of a high-powered company has potential problems predicated on both personality and the capabilities of the management team. The analyst must see the team for its cooperation, not its dissension.

When a company has the only water hole in the desert for 200 miles around, a manager doesn't need a degree from the Harvard Business School to know how to sell water. But most companies function in a competitive economy. The history of American business is laden with managers of major companies who made the wrong decision. A failure to move with the market quickly reduced companies like *WordPerfect* once an industry leader, into such deep trouble that many are now in the hands of other companies. The marketing skill of Microsoft captured the legal market for word processing from *WordPerfect*. *Staples* and *Office Depot,* office supply chains that were at one time competitive, changed course because the management of *Staples* was profoundly sound, and the management of *Office Depot* was less so. *Staples* easily acquired *Office Depot,* expanded its operation, and reduced competition in key markets.

The managers of the large corporation are highly visible. Their efforts and activities and triumphs and failures are trumpeted regularly in the business press. It's the smaller company that needs to be better known by analysts and brokers and prospective investors. It's here that the art of investor relations has its greatest opportunity.

THE BOARD OF DIRECTORS

For decades, boards of directors were, to the public, like poor relatives. Present, but not counting for much in the public arena. With notable exceptions—they are, by definition, the guiding force of a company, with power to hire or fire the CEO—they have traditionally been comprised of cronies, of relatives and friends, of lesser members of the management team. And generally toothless. No more. Sarbanes-Oxley put an end to that. As delineated in Chapter 3, the locus of power now shifts to the board, with strictures about its composition and its powers.

For the investor relations professional, demonstrating the efficacy and integrity of the board, and its conformity to the rules of Sarbanes-Oxley, is a major responsibility.

CREDIBILITY

It is absolutely imperative, for success in the capital markets, for a management team to build a record of consistent openness and truthfulness. Any misrepresentation will not only be readily found out, but will reverberate throughout the financial community like a lion's roar. Furthermore, the number of eyes on a public company are many and keen. A public company is under constant scrutiny. It can take only one disgruntled employee and one astute analyst to topple a corporate empire. Corporate chicanery has a way of gathering heft, until the company falls under the weight of it. Any corporate executive who thinks he or she can deal with the investing public by misrepresenting facts or by refusing to disclose pertinent material necessary for judging his company will not long succeed in the capital markets.

Sarbanes-Oxley, remember, was enacted to a large degree to build credibility, and a large measure of the investor relations professional's task is to project those factors that exude credibility, such as compliance with the strictures of Sarbanes-Oxley.

It's in the area of management analysis, particularly where credibility is involved, that the investor relations professional functions best as an advocate. Numbers can say a great deal in themselves, although they don't always say the same things to different people. The judgment of management, on the other hand, is subjective, and responds well to strong investor relations guidance and support. The investor relations professional should provide the appropriate information when it's appropriate, and not wait for the market to do it.

How, then, is credibility engendered and sustained? One can hardly stand before an audience and say, "This is what I want you to think about me." A company president can hardly stand in front of an audience of security analysts and boast of his or her abilities.

It's good form, on the other hand, for the president to describe, in speaking and writing, the company's management team as being excellent, forward-looking, and skilled. But why should he or she be believed? It's true that some corporate leaders are clean-cut, strong-jawed, and clear-eyed—obviously exciting and believable men and women—at least at the moment they are talking. Other extraordinarily competent corporate leaders are shy, reticent, introspective, and poor public speakers. Some of the most striking photos of chief executive officers appearing in annual reports show leaders of vision and forcefulness, obviously the kind of people in whom widows and orphans should invest their faith and savings. Training corporate executives in public speaking, dress, and television presence is now a big business.

In fact, credibility is a function of three things—corporate performance, consistent truth, and a willingness to deal forthrightly with the public and those who analyze securities in behalf of the public.

PROJECTING MANAGEMENT AS CREDIBLE

The most insightful gauge of management is a personal assessment of integrity and credibility, and this is important. The most tangible gauge of management is still track record. How successfully has management performed? What has it achieved in the growth of the company? How has it survived and dealt with problems? What opportunities has it seized upon and how did it capitalize on them? How has management restructured itself to meet changes in its corporation and its environment?

These and other elements of management capability are projected in real ways. The history of the company, however brief, can be told in terms of management decisions. *"When we realized that the next decade would see a population growth in the number of women between the ages of twenty-eight and thirty-five, we decided to design a special line of sportswear and merchandise it to that group."*

"When we recognized that we were just a few years away from market saturation for our product, we began to explore feasible areas of diversification into products the design and production of which were within our experience and existing capabilities to exploit."

"As our company reached the hundred million dollar mark, we recognized the need for broadening the management base, expanding middle management, and changing the nature of our management reporting systems. Three executives who couldn't comply had to be replaced by people who were better prepared to make appropriate changes."

"As we recognized that the average age of our management team was approaching fifty, we began a recruiting and training program to develop the people who would ultimately be our successors. This has resulted in . . ."

PROJECTING THE FACTS

Yet another way in which management can project itself is to clearly and authoritatively present facts about its company. Consider the erudite company president, surrounded by his or her executive vice-president and vice-president of finance, who recites facts and figures about his company's operation, clearly delineates its present financial structure and its plans for future growth, and obviously has a grasp of his industry and the economy at large. That CEO is much more likely to inspire confidence and credibility than the company president who merely recites, either by rote or from the printed page, material that has already appeared in his annual report, who never lets other members of the management team speak, and who limits the spotlight to himself or herself alone.

The CEO who demonstrates the ways in which the management base has been broadened to meet the growing needs of the company, and who is constantly divesting responsibilities by delegating them to other able people, inspires infinitely more faith than the president of a company who is obviously a one-person band and keeps everything to him or herself, regardless of the number of underlings. The future of a one-person company is no greater than the length of the president's arm, and every analyst knows it.

The CEO who clearly demonstrates the steps that have been taken to comply with Sarbanes-Oxley, in every aspect, including the composition of the board of directors and its audit committee, goes a long way towards inspiring trust.

ANALYZING PLANS

Yet another intangible in which corporate evaluation must be made is the company's own plans. Any analyst with twelve minutes experience has learned to make a distinction between plans and dreams, even though dreams occasionally come true. There are, after all, business people named Gates, Redstone, Dell and Buffet.

Fortunately, the experiences of the past decade have sharply diminished the number of corporate leaders who attempt to pass their dreams as valid projections or plans. It should be recognized by both management and investor relations professionals that the acoustics of Wall Street are magnificent, particularly for bad news or direct misrepresentations. Certainly, it behooves the investor relations professional to lead management to the path of clarity, cogency, and credibility.

What is specifically of the essence here are the legitimate and carefully formulated plans and projections of a company that express more than just its wishes for the future, but are rather the blueprint and road map of company policy for continued profitability, expansion, and growth. The future is, after all, what analysts are concerned with. They know what the present is and what the past was. They may find the management of a company to be charming, sincere, bright, intelligent, highly motivated, ambitious, and trustworthy. But as analysts, they must make an assessment of how these virtues are going to be applied to add shareholder value.

WHAT PLANS MEAN

The CEO of a company with $1 million in sales may have dreams of heading a billion dollar multinational corporation, but may not have the foggiest idea of how to increase sales to $2 million. On the other hand, a CEO who recognizes the potential in certain aspects of biochemistry is planning to expand existing marketing and production capabilities to meet that potential, who hopes to supplement that capability with an acquisition or two, and who recognizes the limitations of his ability to finance those plans, should clearly delineate his or her corporate ideas. The CEO should recognize publicly the dimensions of the potential market, the need to divest certain unprofitable operations, however painful and without emotional consideration, the ways he or she intends to finance the growth and how much it's expected to cost, the kind of management changes he or she is going to have to make, the kind of economic climate in which he or she expects to function, and the down-side risks.

In some cases the plans available for the analysts to consider are relatively simple and unsophisticated. "We are planning to grow through a program of acquisitions and our experience in the past has demonstrated that we can do this. This is the kind of acquisition we are planning to make, this is how we are going to buy the companies, this is the size company we are looking at." And so on and so on. Most of the factors, management is saying, are there for the analysis.

Or so it would seem. There are still many judgments to be made as to the validity of the program. One company in the office cleaning services business had a very simple concept and seemed to have the capabilities to fulfill that concept. It was in an industry made up of predominately smaller privately held companies. The company simply went around the country combining the smaller companies into the larger one. Cash flow was good up to a point. It was an industry that management knew and understood well and seemed capable of managing. The stock was selling at a reasonable multiple, and there was enough available at the right price to allow a considerable amount of it to be used as currency for making the acquisitions, and the banks and the institutions were in a mood to be generous. It worked very well for a while, and every analyst following the company could visualize the successful configuration of both tangibles and intangibles. But then the acquisition momentum outpaced both the ability to manage the rapidly growing company and to finance the continued growth. The company fell on its face. It had to sell off some of its properties in order to revitalize its balance sheet and make payments on its debt, and finally went bankrupt.

THE CAUTIONS OF CORPORATE PLANNING

Corporate planning is itself a very complex business. At best, even supported by sophisticated thinking and computer models, it's precarious. Necessary, but still precarious. Today's commerce and industry move at so rapid a pace, and are interrelated with so many new factors, that traditional planning approaches become obsolete very quickly.

To distinguish the dream from the plan requires as much luck as skill, especially because so many unanticipated random events can substantially alter the best devised plans. New technology. New competitors. New regulatory controls and antitrust rulings. Some larger companies—*IBM, Microsoft, Disney, General Motors, General Electric* with its 400 strategic planners at headquarters, and *Coca-Cola*—have a far greater (but not absolute) capability to control their economic environment, and do plan more effectively than does the smaller company. As significant factors in their industries, companies like *IBM, Coca-Cola,* and *General Electric* receive little surprise from labor. Moreover, they have vast sources of input of economic information, not only domestically but worldwide. They have staff experts to both gather and interpret material, and relationships in every corner of the world. And yet, *IBM,* which once controlled a lion's share of its market, had the wherewithal to finance any reasonable plan, had the scope and diversity to offset and survive most economic swings, and had the marketing capability to expand and develop new markets, found itself swamped in it's market by *Compaq* and other computer manufacturers that were little more than a decade old. The market changed abruptly, and *IBM,* with all its resources, didn't, until new management reassessed its market and its products, and restored the company to its former glory. The same thing happened to *Compaq,* but it didn't quite turn around. It was acquired by H-P.

In other words, when *General Electric,* or any company of comparable size, develops a one-year or a five-year or a ten-year plan for its growth, it does it with infinitely more certainty than one applies to planning next Sunday's picnic.

THE SMALLER COMPANY

If a vast and sophisticated corporate machine like *General Motors* could fail in its corporate planning, caught unawares by the Japanese auto manufacturers, or an *IBM,* in the face of burgeoning computer technology, can be rocked back on its heels by newer and smaller companies, what can an analyst expect of a company a fraction of their size? A small company can blueprint, to a certain degree, its market opportunities and its plans to seize those opportunities, its capital expansion and the means for financing it, the normal growth patterns, and so on. Some of these plans may be perfectly valid, but not in an unforeseeable economic climate. Other plans may be reasonable, but perhaps not for the management as it is presently constituted. The projections may be unrealistic in terms of potential shortages of raw materials or foreseeable problems in distribution patterns and so on. The smaller company may at best have a fine grasp of its own operation and its industry, but its input in terms of the larger economic context or facilities for capitalization down the line are sharply limited, and the company is, of course, more likely to be buffeted in a rough economic sea than is the large corporation. This is the very element that gives a greater appearance of stability to the giant company—the so-called blue-chip stock. The same elements that portend stability and reliability for long-term performance for the larger company are the elements that make it easier for the larger company to plan for the longer range.

There is among analysts a skepticism that was ingrained following the glorious years of the 1960s, the glorious late 70s, and for those following the energy industry, the glorious 1980–1981. The anxiety at the turn of the 21st century was palpable, following the tech stock failure and the scandals. Too many corporate leaders saw the world as a boundless cornucopia and were free in their declarations of a utopian future for their companies. They had, after all, achieved marvelous records so far. The names of a very large number of these people still come to the mind of too many analysts for them to believe any projection of glory that is not specifically documented in terms of how those plans are to be accomplished, predicated upon a record of achievement and comparable activities. Today, some analysts even want to see contingency plans as well.

It is precisely these elements that the analyst must assess as part of the job to determine the ability of the company to generate a profit on the invested dollar in the near, medium, and long-range future.

COMMUNICATING THE PLAN

Perhaps the most sensitive aspect of investor relations is communicating plans to the financial community. Credibility—projecting the plan believ-ably—is only one part of the problem. The more significant aspect is the ret-icence of management to expose plans—even those that will redound to the credit of the CEO and the company.

There are two reasons for this, neither of them totally irrational. One is competitive. In a highly competitive environment, one doesn't give up the element of surprise, any more than would a general in warfare. The other is the fear of litigation in a highly litigious society.

The problem is that the management of a public company has to bal-ance these risks against the risk of losing shareholder confidence. And even that problem is complex, in the face of the rash of corporate fraud in 2000 and the following years.

There are tangible approaches.

- Plans can be specific to concepts, but general to specifics. You can say, "We are putting $10 million into research on a new formula we've developed that we think may offer a cure for the common cold." That is specific. What is general is that you've not identified the formula. You can say, "We intend to address the growing market for digital com-munication," which is a specific generality, without defining the prod-uct technology you're going to use. Or even the market segment you're going after. These are realistic and valid intentions, and without giving away competitive information, you've established a management defi-nition of the company's future.

- You can realistically assess the company's market share. If your company has the lion's share of market, and a toehold into your future, then exposing more about your plans is less dangerous than it would be if you were a minor player, threatening to eat the lion's lunch.
- You can realistically assess the danger of exposing at least enough of your plans to give analysts and investors a sense of clear headed direction. Too often, reticence is unwarranted. What competitors can do with your plans is sometimes like the man who read a book on tightrope walking. He knew everything about tightrope walking except how to do it.
- And ultimately, you can recognize the fact that what you're really after is not simply detailing your plans, but giving analysts and investors a sense of the directions in which the company is going; a reason to believe in its future as a vehicle for appreciating the investment dollar

Much of these approaches are valid for anticipating and attempting to avoid litigation as well. There is an old legal maxim that it only takes a few dollars to file a lawsuit, but the best defense against a suit is to be able to go into court with clean hands.

There is also to be considered the natural friction between lawyers and those who must communicate. Lawyers tend to believe that the less you say in public, the less they can use against you in court, and so, they counsel, say nothing. The communicator believes that the more you say, the better you're known and understood.

Realistically, the balance must be between intelligent and rational caution, and the need to continue to be viable in the marketplace. If each side of the equation recognizes and accepts the needs of the other, there is usually mutual accommodation.

An example of how plans may be safely explained may be seen when Campbell Soup Co. announced to a group of analysts that, to accelerate slow sales growth, the company would take a one-time $160 million charge for a reorganization that included eliminating low-margin brands and cutting almost 700 jobs. This, said the company chairman, would lead to sales growth of about 8% a year, and earnings growth that would be somewhat higher than the company had achieved in recent years. Plants would be closed, advertising would be increased, and marginal operations would be divested. This kind of announcement may be construed to make these points about delineating plans...

- The company was showing that it was taking a bold step for the future.
- There was nothing in the details of the plan, as announced, to give advantage to competitors.
- It showed investors that it was not afraid to take bold steps to put the company on a new growth path.
- It showed investors a management firmly in control of its future and its destiny.

And besides, your plan may work.

MODERN PORTFOLIO THEORY

No view of contemporary analysis can be complete without at least a passing acquaintance with *Modern Portfolio Theory*—MPT. MPT, simply, is a scientific approach to understanding the market value of a security.

While there is very little a company can do, beyond dealing with analytic fundamentals, to influence portfolio analysis using Modern Portfolio Theory, the increasing use of MPT warrants at least a minimal understanding of it.

Essentially, Modern Portfolio Theory is predicated on a concept that the degree of investment risk should be measured in terms of potential reward for that risk. But it also takes as its premise the concept that the greater the range of uncertainty about a stock, the greater the risk.

Portfolio diversification is not a new idea, nor is any form of spreading risk. The aim here, though, is not merely to diversify, but to do so with a balance of stocks with varying degrees of risk, and therefore varying likelihood of performance, so that the average uncertainty of the total portfolio—and therefore the average of the portfolio's risk—is diminished in relation to potential return.

For example, in a two-stock portfolio, if both stocks perform in the same way in response to the market itself, there is no real diversification. If, however, each responds differently to market forces, then you do have diversification. But not necessarily the best diversification, unless the potential performance of one effectively hedges, or acts opposite to and offsets, the potential performance of the other.

Measuring potential performance, and thereby potential risk-return, is done with a series of complex mathematical functions, but the basis is still a judgment of fundamental analysis of the elements of a company's potential. Beyond that, however, portfolio analysis becomes complex.

The aim is to build an *efficient* portfolio, one in which the balance of potential performance of all the stocks in the portfolio is one of minimum uncertainty. Taken into account are two major elements of risk—the risk in the individual stock and the risk inherent in the market itself, keeping in mind that not all stocks react or perform in the same way in response to the market at any given moment. Using the Standard & Poor's 500 Stock Price Index as a basis, price fluctuations—the measure of risk used—are broken down into the two risk elements (market and individual stock). The statistical technique, regression analysis, is used to measure the potential risk. A complex mathematical technique, it measures functional relationships between two or more variables, particularly where a variable (such as a price/earnings ratio) is measured against another variable (such as a market index).

Put simply, the term *beta* is used to indicate the measure of a stock's volatility, relative to the volatility of the market during the same period. The higher the *beta*, the higher the volatility; the lower the *beta* the more stable. A *beta* of one means that the stock performs exactly as the market does.

The term *alpha* is used to indicate the measure of average rate of return, in the same period, independent of the market return.

A portfolio that matches the *alpha* and *beta* of the S&P 500 should—and generally does—perform about the same as the S&P Index, and indeed many index funds (funds designed to match the Standard & Poor's 500) have been started based on the concept. However, there is a serious question in the minds of many professional investors, particularly institutional investors, whether indexed return, rather than one that outperforms the market, is sufficient.

In the several years since the theory was developed by the statistician Dr. Harry M. Markowitz, it has grown in popularity among analysts. But even its strongest advocates warn that it is a theory with a great deal yet to be developed and proven, and more significantly, that it is only one tool of many that should be used by analysts. It does not portend, in the foreseeable future, eliminating all analysts and replacing them with computers.

LIVING WITH THE ANALYTICAL PROCESS

There is no part of investor relations in which more is demanded of the investor relations professional than dealing with analysts. Truth is of the essence, as is vivid communications. And keep in mind at all times Regulation FD.

Advocacy is a major role as well. How, then, does the investor relations professional balance advocacy with truth, especially when the truth is not particularly favorable? The answer is that, as simplistic as it may sound, truth pays better dividends, sometimes in the long run, than does misdirection or deception. Once again, it must be recognized that the acoustics of Wall Street are magnificent, and the truth will emerge sooner or later. If the truth doesn't square with the story being told, then the company loses more than if it had told the truth in the first place.

Even in advocacy, truth is the best weapon against adversity. The company, the shareholders, Wall Street, and the public at large are the winners.

CHAPTER 7

Dealing with the Business and Financial Media

On and Off the Record to Get It Right

It would be impossible, following the period of economic turmoil at the beginning of the century, for the financial media not to be affected in both its attitudes and its structure. This technical, communication, and economic maelstrom has created a new media environment that, in many ways, is radically different from its predecessors. And, fortunately, is in many ways the same.

Where once business and financial news was, for the most part, mundane and of interest to only a small segment of the media audience, it now dominates the news in all media, and has created a new generation of professional financial journalists. Business news, in the past, was buried in the back pages of most local newspapers, and was, for the most part, written for an economic cognoscenti. Now, with a rash of business and accounting scandals, and with the burgeoning stock ownership, business news is front page and prime time news. Business news has a new, huge, and demanding audience. And more media to deliver it.

This is not surprising, in view of factors that are now part of our economic environment...

- The audience for business and economic news is now vast The number of investors, whether individual, through mutual funds, or with 401(k) and other pension plans, has grown substantially in recent years. More people in this country—some fifty percent of the population—have a stake in the stock market than ever before. And because of the relationship between the market and the economy, more non-professional investors have become enthusiastic economy watchers.

- The number of major companies involved in financial scandals has resulted in the loss of thousands of jobs, untold thousands of dollars in pension benefits, and of billions of dollars that had been invested in the stock of the many major companies thrown into disaster. Outsourcing jobs abroad has added to the unemployment numbers. To those who have lost jobs or life savings, the business news is no longer academic. It's now mainstream.

- The growth of the internet, and its maturity as a conduit of news, has brought a new dimension of communications, and particularly of news, to the financial community, both professional and individual. Where once the *Wall Street Journal,* the *New York Times,* and a few other big city dailies dominated the business and financial news scene, business news is now on the front pages of smaller newspapers, and is featured prominently in radio, television, and the internet. Increasingly, the internet as a source of business news is now on a par with more traditional media, for its breadth and depth as well as its immediacy.

- The thirst for business news, in all media, has led to a new generation of sophisticated financial news reporters. There are now more MBA's in the newsrooms of newspapers, broadcast media and internet web sites and blogs than ever before. They are producing some truly thoughtful business journalism. Where once business news was simply another beat for staff reporters, business journalism is now a profession on its own. Where once the business-literate journalist was a rare individual, that tribe has now increased substantially.

- At the same time, there has been a shift in the mechanisms of news delivery. Where once the newspaper dominated as a major source of business news, broadcast media and the internet now share the stage and gets equal, and sometimes greater, attention. Moreover, this new hunger for business news has bred the superstar... the media personality reporting business news. It would be inaccurate, however, not to mention the downside. The need to fill time and space, and to compete successfully for audience in a fulsome arena, also breed a plethora of talking heads—so-called experts who don't always have something to say, but say it anyway.

In the old media world, just a decade ago, outlets for business news were limited to a relatively few business publications, and to a much lesser extent, to broadcast media. Other than publications like the *Wall Street Journal* and the big city dailies, business news commanded less space than the garden club news. An individual who wanted to follow the tape or the Dow Jones Newswire had to go to a brokerage office or private club.

Gone now, in financial media (with notable exceptions) is the beat reporter who covered police news one day and business news another. Gone is the general business editor who was little more than a tape reader, with little knowledge of the dynamics and economics of business.

But then, with stock ownership limited to an elite few, there was little audience for business journalism. And with relatively small audiences, there were relatively few outlets.

The growth of stock ownership, the sustained prosperity of the 1990's, and ultimately, the new outlets for business news changed all that.

Fortunately, the old standards of good business journalism remain, but with new sophistication. Many of the second-rate puff-piece publications are gone. But now there is a vast array of new publications offering substantive economic, business, and stock market news for every investor, large or small. There are knowledgeable and important professional television and radio business broadcasters, and cable channels and programs dedicated to business news, stock market reports, and in-depth company information. There are business reporters who are media stars, with ratings in the same class as network anchors. And no longer is it necessary to sit in front of the tape in a brokerage office. The cable station CNBC runs the tape, in real time, every day.

Then there is the internet, through which any investor can learn as much about a company's business as any analyst may know, particularly since the activation of SEC Regulation FD. Lacking for the non-professional investor is only the analyst's access to management, but that's OK— the CEO is likely to be interviewed on a cable TV program.

And now there are blogs—*Web logs*—produced by individuals or even corporations, that report personal opinions as well as news,

THE NEW BUSINESS JOURNALIST

To a degree large enough to be outstanding, the new business journalists are as knowledgeable and professional as any security analyst. The new journalists knows how to write and report well. They know the right questions to ask, and are not afraid to ask them.

The new business journalist frequently covers a specific industry, and in larger media, a specific company or group of companies. This means two things—there is intensive expertise and focus, and there is often direct access to a company's managers, without going through the investor relations specialist. Katie Vukas of the international public relations firm Cubitt, Jacobs & Prosek, calls it disintermediation, which puts a new twist on investor relations, particularly for more prominent companies.

Where once the personal pronoun—*I*—was completely taboo in journalism, it now appears with increasing frequency in news stories, and more so in features. The byline journalist is a celebrity. The new journalist is not very susceptible to *spin* (to deliberately put a favorable face on the news, or to direct the journalists attention to specific aspects of the news)—he or she knows better.

No general news matches business news as a cause for action by the reader. News of an earthquake in another part of the world or of the marriage of a movie star moves few people to action. News of a business event—even one that might not specifically concern an individual, leads to an action. That action may be the purchase or sale of a stock, or a decision to retrench on eating out. But business and economic news causes action.

Significantly, as the breadth and ubiquity of business news has grown, so too has the definition of business news altered, as has, to a large extent, the delivery mechanisms and the techniques of dealing with the media (of which more further on).

THE COMPETITION FOR NEWS

Consider that despite the increase in media outlets and coverage, the amount of news that any medium can accommodate on any given day is finite. There is only so much space, so much time, and in the internet, there are the limits of attention span. Thus, the competition for that time and space is keen, and can be won only with a full understanding of how modern media works, and with a professionalism equal to that of the best journalists. If you measure the news you have to impart about your company against the news of an Arthur Andersen's demise, a Martha Stewart conviction, or a WorldCom or HealthSouth fraud, you get a different sense of proportion. And yet, beyond the legal disclosure requirements, the value of being covered by the media as an investor relations tool is immeasurable.

Effective media relations is integral to a sound investor relations program. It's also complex, and requires skill and attention.

HOW NEWS AFFECTS THE STOCK MARKET

A significant aspect of news is the way in which it affects the capital markets. The news that the chairman of the Federal Reserve Bank publicly suggests that there are signs of economic recovery reflects almost instantly in the stock market. The market reacts when the U.S. Food and Drug Administration approves a drug, and when an airplane manufacturer gets a major contract. It reacts when an audit fraud is uncovered, and when a company has a research breakthrough. And the market seems to react to every election, regardless of which party wins, and to wars, and to violent weather in a bread basket area of the country. The stock market, reacting to the news of the day (or more appropriately, the news of the minute), can be a nervous cat.

The market certainly reacts to an event, and to the news of it. The financial chicanery of the Enrons and WorldComs, the failures of the accounting profession and the dramatic demise of the giant accounting firm Arthur Andersen, were a reality of inevitable newsworthiness. No investor relations or public relations professional was necessary to get those stories in the paper. But not all business news is as substantial as these great disasters. There is lesser news that is consequential to the dynamics of the financial markets. The difference is that in dealing with financial media, this lesser news must sometimes be made clear to editors in all media, who might not readily understand the relationship of the news to the investment decision. Therein lies the role of the investor relations communicator.

One thing is certain, then. The market—the stock market as well as all other money markets—does respond to news.

In their classic book on the subject, *News and the Market*, Frederick C. Klein and John A. Prestbo, two *Wall Street Journal* reporters, explored that relationship in great detail. They say, "It certainly makes sense to believe that the stock market responds to the news. Movements of the market as a whole and of the stocks that make it up spring from the decisions of thousands of investors. These people, be they steely-eyed fund managers on Wall Street or little old ladies in Dubuque—read the newspapers, watch television and so on, and presumably are affected by what they see and hear. If the United States economy seems to be functioning smoothly, it stands to reason that they will feel well disposed towards sharing in the bounty. If the opposite conditions obtain, a bank account or hole in the ground might seem more secure."

In his very popular book, *A Random Walk on Wall Street,* Princeton Professor Burton Malkiel covered many theories of stock market analysis and relates virtually all significant stock movement to news. Both books deal with time lag—the time between the reporting of news and the reaction to it in the stock market—an extremely important factor. The company issues a quarterly release that shows earnings lower than those of the same period for the prior year. The stock shows no motion or perhaps even advances a little. This frequently means that the market has anticipated the reduced earnings and sold off in proportion to them, or that the reduction is smaller than had been anticipated and that other events, or a new outlook, warrant stock purchase. The important thing is that all segments of the capital markets, from the individual investor to the manager of a major fund or trust department to the lending officer of a bank, are responsive to news.

Malkiel dealt with the *efficient market* theory, a basis of which is that the entire market is privy to the same information and so reacts accordingly as one. Critics point out, however, that the market isn't universally privy to the same news, particularly in smaller companies (which is why we sometimes have a two-tier market), and not everybody interprets the same news in the same way (which is why we have an auction market).

With the vast array of sources of data—company, industry, economy, and so fourth—efficient market theory is diluted by those who access the news. This is both a potential weakness in efficient market theory, and an opportunity for the investor relations practitioner. The company that explains itself best to investors is the one that wins the competition for investment capital.

THE SALUTARY EFFECTS OF NEWS

Obviously, imparting news about any company can have several immediate salutary effects, even if the news is adverse.

- The news itself adds further information for the investment decision.
- News that openly discusses the company can add credibility to all company reports.

- The publication of the news keeps the company name prominent in the minds of those who make investment or lending decisions—certainly important in an arena in which the competition is keen for not only capital, but for attention as well. This is perhaps the most significant point, since in the competition for capital those companies that are best known and understood are those likeliest to succeed.

This is why news, and the dissemination of it, is so important a part of the investor relations process. Its materiality and ability to affect stock market decisions is also why it so readily falls within the purview of the SEC and the exchanges.

HOW NEWS IS RECEIVED BY THE FINANCIAL COMMUNITY

What is harder to fathom, then, is the way in which any news—and all news—will be received by the financial community.

First, it should be recognized that since news itself is relative, most news is viewed in a larger context. Nothing is absolute. A report of an SEC review of a company's accounting practices is bad news even if the company is otherwise profitable, and not such bad news if the results of the review are clean. If the CEO is indicted for fraud that's bad news, unless the company is profitable and the rot doesn't affect anybody but the CEO. In other words, good things and bad things that happen to a company may not necessarily, in the eyes of the market, be good or bad news of itself. For the investor trying to fathom the future, all news is mitigated by other news.

Second, it must be recognized that the nature of the capital markets is such that because of mass psychology, there is never simply a reaction to news (particularly if it's not anticipated)—there is only an overreaction. Again, the market is *people*, and the reaction is a human, not a mechanical, one. The market almost invariably recoils at bad news in anticipation of the worst possible consequences. It's just as likely to overreact, in a burst of optimism, in the other direction at the announcement of good news. The problem is that the overreaction is immediate, and the adjustment to reality, if it comes, is slower, sometimes barely perceptible in the short range, and frequently spread over time.

Beyond that, the reaction depends as much upon the type of news as the news itself. Some events, for example, are anticipated and then discounted by the market. While it can be tremendously frustrating to a company president to announce record earnings for a quarter or a year only to see virtually no reaction in his stock—or perhaps a reaction on the down side—the fact is that his earnings have probably been anticipated by those who follow the company. Or it could mean that forces outside the company could be adversely coloring the meaning of the news. Then the announcement itself is not news at all, but merely an affirmation of what had been anticipated. This, incidentally, is part of the problem with projecting earnings. If analysts anticipate earnings of $1.50 per share, they predicate their recommendations on that. When earnings of $1.50 are announced, the effect of the earnings on the price of the stock has already been taken into consideration, and, in effect, the good news is no news at all. If the analysts have anticipated and projected earnings of $1.50 and the actual figure comes out to be $1.45, this can be a disappointment, with an adverse effect on the stock price, even though the $1.45 may be a record. Nobody ever said the market was rational.

The rules of disclosure under Regulation FD assure that material information is disseminated to investors and other relevant parties on a timely basis, affording equal opportunity to all, and unwarranted advantage to none. This means, theoretically, that everybody has the same news at the same time.

Even this is an oversimplification. Since the news of record earnings can be qualified by other factors, such as an understanding that the earnings are derived from inventory profits and not improved operations, analysts know that the high earnings in any one accounting period are not an accurate reflection of the company's overall performance.

We now know, as well, that the nature and meaning of news—in fact, of all data—changes the moment it's accessed. It takes on the coloration of the reader or listener, and its meaning is adapted by the reader or listener's personal screen. And if an action is taken as a result of the news (e.g. a stock is bought or sold) the meaning or essence of the original news is altered.

The purpose of the Sarbanes-Oxley Act of 2002 is to attempt to assure the validity and integrity of a company's financial information, so that an investor may more accurately assess a company's financial position. This contributes to the texture of the news in two ways—it increases the likelihood that the financial information supplied to the media is more accurate, and by virtue of the stringency of Sarbanes-Oxley and SEC rules and regulations, it makes the media and the investor more comfortable with information from the company. For the investor relations professional, it adds the opportunity to build credibility with the media by projecting the company's compliance with the law, and therefore its integrity.

WHAT IS NEWS?

For all that and all that, what indeed is news? Is it merely a report of the events of the day? Is it really objective? What makes information news?

Obviously, to be newsworthy, a fact must have some measure of impact on its audience. If a CEO buys a small sailboat, it's hardly news with an impact—news that matters to a great many people. If the same CEO, whose company's profits are down and whose stock is deep in the tank, buys an 80 foot yacht or personal jet with company money, that's a fact with impact. That's news that may be material, which means it may affect the investor's buy or sell decision.

As seen in Chapter 3, the concept of materiality is important. If that CEO bought the yacht with his wife's inherited money, it's not material to the company's operation, and is therefore not likely to affect the investor's interest in the company. If he bought it with company money, the news is surely material, since it will indeed affect the investor's view of the company, and therefore its stock price.

In fact, all news is relative, because the value of all information is defined not by the source of the news, but by its receivers, whether editors or readers. Every day the editor in any medium must review all reported events of that day and make a subjective judgment as to which of those events will concern or interest readers sufficiently to warrant the allocation of rare and precious space or time. On any given day the news of the bankruptcy of a company of, say, the size of a Fortune 500 company is likely to garner more editorial interest than will the news of a very large privately held company merging with another large privately held company. This in turn will preempt in importance the decision of a company to build a $500 million plant. And this in turn will preempt the news of record earnings for a $50 million company (unless the company is the major industry of a small town in which its success or failure affects a great many local jobs). Lower down on the list is the routine appointment of a new vice-president. Yet sometimes, if not very much has happened in town that day, the news of a joint venture between two relatively small companies may be the most exciting thing the newspaper has to report as business news.

News is also subjective. What is major business news to one editor may not be to another, depending upon each editor's understanding of the medium's audience. Not to be overlooked, too, are the medium's political position, or the bias of a journalist.

The real nature and meaning of news may, ultimately, be elusive—even phantom—in its propensity to change shape and meaning. The facts inherent in any news change in relationship to other facts, and to contexts that are dynamic. Even as mundane a fact as an earnings statement has, to a medium, a meaning that an editor may judge in terms of an economic environment, a value judgment based upon a company's industry, a statement that reflects its potential to change the course of the stock market, and so forth. Note, for example, the news of a profit beyond that projected by analysts for a chip manufacturer, following a period of losses in the computer industry. That news becomes more than the fact of a profit report—it becomes a harbinger.

The art in garnering space or time in any medium begins with understanding the meaning of news, followed by understanding the nature of a publication and its audience, followed by writing to the mediums own professional standards.

The important consideration for the investor relations professional is that in reporting a fact, context, perhaps more than the fact, makes it news.

THE AUDIENCES FOR NEWS

There are actually three audiences for business news. One consists of those who already know the subject company, either as investors or potential investors, or as analysts or brokers following it for one reason or another. Another is the larger segment of the financial community, which is interested in business news as a context for making further businesses decisions beyond investing alone. Another is the general public, for whom business news may be interesting, but not necessarily crucial to their everyday lives.

The feature material about a company or an executive that appears in the vast range of business publications, from *Fortune* magazine to the business section of the Sunday *New York Times,* and from business and trade periodicals, offers a distinctive point of view of a company. There's no question that frequent coverage makes a vast difference. With some 18,000 plus companies traded, obviously those that are better known get the greatest attention from the investment community. When two companies are performing equally well, the difference between the higher stock price or price/earnings ratio of one company as compared to another is a function of its being better known and understood by a broader segment of the investment community. For the better known company, the simplest positive news announcement will have beneficial results.

The broader reputation engendered by feature material can stem either from media recognition of the sheer brilliance or uniqueness of a company's performance, or it can just as validly be the result of an organized and carefully executed financial publicity program. While the likelihood of the media discovering a superior company on its own, without the help of an investor relations or public relations professional, exists, it rarely happens for companies other than those in the Fortune 500 or 1000. No media staff, in any medium, is large enough, nor are that many reporters experienced enough, to discover companies serendipitously. For major national or international companies, the trade and business media frequently assign reporters to cover the companies as a beat. For the lesser company, news of value to the business and investing community rarely surfaces on its own. The exception, of course, is when scandal is involved. When the SEC or U.S. Department of Justice is involved, no public relations or investor relations professional is needed to make the news.

The aim of positive media recognition is to draw attention to a company repeatedly. Repetition is absolutely essential. While a single media appearance of an announcement about a company may gladden the heart of its president, if it's isolated and the company has never been heard of before and is not heard of again, its effect on any segment of the financial community that's not directly involved with the company is fleeting.

There is another major distinction between the news announcement, such as the earnings report or the report of a merger, and the feature article in *Fortune, Forbes,* or *Business Week,* or an appearance on CNN or MSNBC. The news announcement may be required by the rules of disclosure of the SEC. As long as the company is large enough to be included in the stock tables of the *Wall Street Journal,* the likelihood is that the announcement will at least be carried over the Dow Jones and Reuters wire services and in the agate line listings in the *Wall Street Journal* and *The New York Times.* This should also be supplemented by fax, direct mail, and internet distribution from the company to investors, analysts, and prospective investors—not everybody you want to reach may be reading the paper that day—or by purchase arrangements for news releases to be published in the corporate reports sections of the several publications that carry them, such as *Barron's, Fortune,* or *Investor's Daily.*

With publicity material, the fact of editorial judgment comes into play—and this remains the purview of the editor, not the subject of the news. The company may only beseech the editor. There is no effective external power beyond that, and the judgment of the editor who must serve the needs of his readers is paramount. In media relations, we propose, but others dispose.

It should also be noted that while news is significant in supporting a stock and the company behind the stock, rare is the news that will, of itself, move a stock. All good news must be disseminated as well through other shareholder communications, all bad news must be dealt with head on, and disseminated as well. This is the role—and the skill—of the investor relations professional.

SPINNING OUT OF CONTROL

Every election campaign produces, among other things, media myths and bad language. During the elections of the last decade, the language was infected by a new myth called *spin control*. The phrase, which broke a speed record in becoming a cliché after the 1988 election, implies that a good media relations practitioner can control the nature and texture of a story in the press—can put the right *spin* on it to get the journalist to tell it the spinner's way.

It's just not so. For all that the myth implies, when it comes to the media, investor relations and public relations specialists may persuade an editor to receive the news, but the editor determines what runs and what doesn't. Thus it was, and thus it always shall be, so long as we have a free press.

But is the telling by the media always accurate? No. Is it always fair? No. Sometimes, despite all of the public relations professionalism, and despite all the cooperation we may offer the press, the story comes out badly. Disaster, dispensed in the aura of a supposedly objective media, doesn't merely strike, it reverberates.

The picture you so carefully and accurately painted is distorted, the wrong people are quoted and the right people are not, the facts are warped and bent beyond recognition, and the whole piece reads as if it were written by your most malicious competitor. Certainly, it will be relished by your every detractor.

THE EXPERTS' ADVICE

Beyond the first scream of outrage, what can you do? Or more significantly, what has been done most effectively by others who have lived through it—and survived?

Perhaps the hardest factor of a negative story to deal with is that most people who are not professional marketers tend to overreact. At one extreme is incredible upset and anger; at the other is casual disdain that says, "So what, no one will believe it." Neither extreme is warranted nor accurate.

The most useful course, then, is to do nothing until you've recovered from your anger. Even doing the right thing in the wrong frame of mind can perpetuate, not cure, the damage. So...

- Don't act precipitously. Think of every action in terms of possible reaction. What seems like a good idea at the moment may be a backfire next week.
- After you've gotten over the emotional impact and the anger, don't think vindictively. You may have to live with that publication again someday, and vindictiveness in any event is not profitable.
- Assess real—not assumed or presumed—damage. That's where you've got to focus your attention. Much assumed damage at first light disappears when the sun comes up. What's left is damage you can deal with.

It's this last point that's crucial to successfully limiting the damage of bad press. Too often, the defense is predicated on imagined damage, in which case the reaction is an overreaction, and causes more damage than the original article.

Experts rarely concern themselves with why it happened. Unless libel is involved, it doesn't really matter. The reporter could have functioned out of ignorance or laziness. Reporters are people, and are not immune to such foibles as preconceived notions that can subvert the professionalism of even the most experienced journalist. There may have been an adverse chemical reaction to somebody in your firm, or a fight at the journalist's home that morning. It fact, it really doesn't matter, because the reason for an adverse story is rarely an element that can be dealt with in damage control.

There are some specific questions to be addressed:

- What does the article really say? Is it bad because it's wrong—or because it's right?
- Is the article distorted because the facts are wrong, or because they are put in a wrong context that distorts the facts?
- What is the real damage? Is it libelous? Misleading enough to cause real business damage? Or just embarrassing?
- Consider the publication. Is it widely read, or will people you care about never see it? (Consider that under certain circumstances, your competitor may want to make a point by sending a reprint of the article, along with a favorable one about himself from the same publication.) What's the publication's reputation for credibility?
- Is the potential damage internal as well as external? Sometimes an unfavorable article can hurt internal morale more than it affects an external perception of the firm.

THE IMPACT FADES QUICKLY

Staying power is an important consideration. How long after publication will the story, or at least its negative aura, linger? Depending upon the publication and the nature of the story, considerably less time than you think. As one experienced marketer put it, the impact fades quickly, but the impression can linger.

Some time ago, a major professional firm was savaged in the press for nepotism. The impact was shocking. In fact, the firm not only lost very little business, but continued to grow. Did the story, on the other hand, contribute to competitive defeats? Hard to say. An impression may have lingered in a prospective client's mind, and contributed to other negatives. But ultimately, the damage was nowhere equal to the impact and shock of the article's first appearance.

RESPONDING TO THE DAMAGE

Assessing the damage accurately allows you to choose the appropriate response. There are, in fact, a number of responses, some, unfortunately, inappropriate. You can:

- Sue, but only if there is real libel and real—and demonstrable—damage. There rarely is.
- Get on the phone and scream at the editor. Good for your spleen, lousy for your future with at least that segment of the press. And you'll never win.
- Write a nasty letter to the publisher. Only slightly better than screaming, but with the same results.

On the other hand, there are some positive things that can be done:

- Avoid defensiveness. Plan positively.
- Warn people. If you know an article is going to appear that might be unfavorable, alert your own people, so that it doesn't come as a surprise.
- Have a plan and a policy, preferably before you need it. This should cover how to deal with the press, who does it and who doesn't, how to deal with client reactions, how to deal with internal reactions. It should cover how calls are handled, who responds and who routes calls to whom, what to say to clients and who says it, and so forth.
- A letter to the editor is important, if only to go on record. But it should be positive, non-vitriolic, and deal only with the facts. It should not sound petulant or defensive.
- Deal with the real damage. If the real damage is in specific segments of the financial community, mount a positive public relations campaign aimed specifically at those segments. If the damage is internal, try to assess the root causes for the negative reaction. It would take a powerful article in a powerful journal to demoralize a firm that's otherwise sound and comfortable with itself.
- Consider how a competitor might use the piece, even within the bounds of propriety. It could be, for example, reprints to a particular segment of the financial community. Offset this with positive publicity to the same segment.

No story is so bad that it should warrant extreme reaction. No publication that's still publishing is so devoid of credibility that some readers won't accept what they read. The role of the professional, trained, and experienced investor relations professional is to maintain perspective, to assess the damage appropriately, and to see that the response is equal to—but does not exceed—the damage.

If bad press meant nothing, then neither would good press, and we know that consistently good press means a great deal. But one story—good or bad—rarely has sufficient impact to seriously aid or damage a company (although a negative story is more titillating than a positive one). Most positive public relations is a consistent series of positive articles, interviews and news stories. If a negative press consists of more than one story, then the problem is usually not the press—it's the subject of the stories.

The perspective of the bad story, then, requires dealing with it as an anomaly. This means dealing with it as a calm and rational business decision. And no business decision, in any context, is ever a sound one if it isn't arrived at rationally and professionally.

AIMS OF FINANCIAL PUBLICITY

In the realm of investor relations, the value of visibility through the media is high and warrants the specific effort that must go into achieving it. Its ultimate aims are . . .

- To achieve and sustain visibility for the company, its management, its products or brands, and its activities.
- To project the company's capabilities in ways that demonstrate its ultimate ability to appreciate the invested dollar.
- To demonstrate specific capabilities about the company—its abilities to earn, the abilities of its management, its research and development, its future plans, its grasp of its industry and markets, its ability to control costs and ultimately increase its margins, and so forth.
- To demonstrate the consistency of the company's performance, as well as the credibility of its management in the veracity of all its representations of the company in the past.

It's rare that a company, by virtue of its positive performance alone, will generate sufficient interest to warrant ongoing and continuous appearances in the financial media. A company in trouble, if the trouble is flagrant and the effect of the trouble is significant enough to a large segment of the financial community, has no problem in getting itself broadly covered by the financial media. Witness Enron, Tyco, HealthSouth, and so forth. Since few companies purposely generate this kind of interest, professional efforts for the healthy company must be used to discern those elements about the company and its operation that are consistently newsworthy and valuable to these publications. This material must be presented to the publications professionally. Financial publicity on a consistent basis is at least a hard sell, best performed by experts, with full knowledge of not only the techniques of dealing with the media, but the individual requirements of each publication. There should also be a basis of experience that warrants credibility with the media for the investor relations practitioner, as well as for the company he represents.

WORKING IN THE NEW MEDIA ENVIRONMENT

In the current media environment, and with the maturity of electronic media and the internet, many of the traditional rules of media relations have metamorphed into new structures. The audience for business news has changed, the media delivering business news has changed, the journalists who cover business news has changed. For the investor relations practitioner, the techniques of working with the media have changed as well.

In the old media world, just a decade ago, outlets for business news were limited to a relatively few business publications, and to a much lesser extent, to broadcast media. Other than publications like the *Wall Street Journal* and the big city dailies, business news commanded less space than the garden club news. An individual who wanted to follow the tape or the Dow Jones Newswire had to go to a brokerage office or private club.

For readers of the general press, other than the big city dailies, there was little expectation of insight beyond local business news, abbreviated wire reports, and truncated stock tables. But then, just a few decades ago, the tribe of active investors was comparatively small.

Gone, in financial media (with notable exceptions) is the beat reporter who covered police news one day and business news another. Gone is the general business editor who was little more than a tape reader, with little knowledge of the dynamics and economics of business. The tribe of knowledgeable, insightful, and professional business journalists, small as it was, could be found only in major financial journals—the *Wall Street Journal, Barron's, Financial World,* the *New York Times,* for example.

But then, with stock ownership limited to an elite few, there was little audience for business journalism. And with relatively small audiences, there were relatively few outlets.

The growth of stock ownership, the sustained prosperity of the 1990's, and ultimately, the new outlets for business news changed all that.

The old standards of good business journalism remain, but with new sophistication. There are a significant number of journalists with MBA's and other relevant degrees. Many of the second-rate puff-piece publications are gone. But now there is a vast array of new publications offering substantive economic, business, and stock market news for every investor, large or small. There are knowledgeable and important professional television and radio business broadcasters, and cable channels and programs dedicated to business news, stock market reports, and in-depth company information. There are business reporters who are media stars, with ratings in the same class as network anchors. And no longer is it necessary to sit in front of the tape in a brokerage office. The cable station MSNBC runs the tape, in real time, every day.

Then there is the internet, through which any investor can learn as much about a company's business as any analyst may know, particularly since the activation of Regulation FD. The ordinary investor may lack only the analyst's access to management, but that's OK—the CEO is likely to be interviewed on a cable TV program.

Weblogs, the personalized web site of an individual or a group, is a new form of journalism that frequently includes business or economic news. As personal sites, they often go beyond journalistic objectivity in expressing opinion or even news. But many weblogs are written by knowledgeable and insightful people. They are growing rapidly in popularity, and must be viewed as viable outlets and sources for economic—and sometimes company—news.

The online journal, such as *Salon* and Microsoft's *Slate,* is now a viable source of information. These online publications are well written, usually by professional journalists, and have become a major news medium. At the same time, both network and cable news organizations are also online with both general and business news. They are now as widely read as their print or television versions, and are increasingly important as a source of business news.

Online web sites, such as *AOL, MSN,* and *Yahoo,* have vast readership, with extensive business coverage, including real time stock quotes. And of course, every major metropolitan daily newspaper, from the *New York Times* to the *Washington Post* to the *Los Angeles Times* carries a full business section online. The *Wall Street Journal* has an online version, as do many other business publications. Search engines, such as *Google,* can summon up vast amounts of information about a company. Dedicated business web sites, such as *The Motley Fool,* offer insights into the workings of Wall Street and listed companies.

Not to be overlooked in the new media is e-mail. E-mail allows not just a single message to be sent between individuals, but the ability to build a virtual community. A group of many analysts, institutional investors, shareholders and others can be reached with a single e-mail. E-mail is also a feedback device. Have a question about a company? Send it by e-mail to the CEO or the CFO or the investor relations officer.

CATEGORIES OF BUSINESS NEWS

Financial and business news generally falls into the following specific categories...

- News released under the Rules of Disclosure of the SEC and the Exchanges. This is financial and other company information deemed material to an investment decision
- *Major news events* beyond routine financial announcements. This is significant company news beyond reporting financial performance. It may be material, or may be just background. Evidence of a potential oil field, neither proven nor exploited, is background. Finding a major pool of oil may be material. This category includes, as well, news of fraud or other white collar crime.
- *Feature material.* This is general background information about a company, such as a discussion of a company's management policies, or a profile of management, or its success in entering new markets. This kind of material can help clarify a company's goals, its management skills, its market potential, and so forth. Favorable feature articles can enhance reputation, and build faith in a company's future. Included in this category are the interviews with key management personnel.
- *Routine announcements,* such as key personnel changes or new product announcements. While this kind of news may not directly affect a company's stock, it serves to keep the company's name before the business and investment public.
- *Inquiries* from, and stories originated by, the media. Increasingly, the media circumvents the investor relations professional to go directly to management. Because there are specific skills in being interviewed

effectively, all company officers should be briefed in these skills well before the phone rings.

RULES FOR WORKING WITH THE FINANCIAL MEDIA

The general rules of disseminating basic material required to be disclosed are essentially simple and mechanical, yet if a professional approach is ignored, the effect will be sharply diminished.

In working with the media—in any medium—the objective of your presentation should always be kept in mind and in focus. The idea is to present the message about your company in the most favorable light, with focus on the key points, and without distorting the truth. This should be kept in mind even when the news is obviously positive. The most successful media relations are those practices that are clearly thought out beforehand.

In dealing with the financial media—or any media for that matter—some simple rules apply universally:

- The ultimate judgment of news value by the media is made by its editors. Even in those publications that cross the line that separates news from advertising, the publisher knows that if his editorial content does not consistently interest readers, the number of readers will diminish, as well as credibility of his publication. This is invariably followed by a cutback in advertising revenue, which is inevitably followed by bankruptcy. A primary factor in any publication, then, is its editorial judgment.
- Each medium is predicated on a different editorial format—for example, *Fortune* magazine does not print routine earnings reports, *Barron's* rarely does personality pieces on corporate heads, and so on. Each broadcast journalist has a different format and approach to the news, in addition to time restraints. Each online publication has its own format and editorial guidelines. The editorial point of view of every medium must be discerned and understood before any approach is made to it. *Do not, under any circumstances, submit material to any medium you haven't carefully read, seen or heard beforehand. You will not only be wasting your time, you will be annoying the journalist and foreclosing future relationships.*
- Competition for news space or air time or internet space is extraordinarily keen. Even though business news coverage is increasing in many

media, editors receive five and ten times as much news as they can possibly publish. Therefore, the form of presentation of news to a medium is extremely important. It must attract attention for its essential news value in the shortest possible time. It must be in a format traditionally acceptable to each medium. Wherever possible, it must be written in a journalistic style acceptable to most editors.

RULES OF DISCLOSURE

The Rules of Disclosure dictate that material information that could affect an investment decision—shall be released as rapidly as possible. These rules have been further reinforced by Regulation FD, by the stringencies of Sarbanes-Oxley, and by the proliferation of new media. The basic objectives of the Rules of Disclosure, however, remain the same—to assure that all investors have equal access to material information at the same time, and that no investor has material information before the general public has it. The Rules of Disclosure are considered satisfied when this information is released, as soon as possible after it's known to management, to the Dow Jones News Service, *Bloomberg,* and *Reuters,* plus the other major wires (*AP* and *UPI*), the company's major local newspapers, the *New York Times,* and the company's exchange or NASD and NASDAQ. What is essential is that the news is released through the broadest possible media spectrum reaching the largest number of investors or potential investors.

This is best achieved by the following procedure:

- *Simultaneous release,* by a PR wire service, computer, fax, telephone, or hand, to Dow Jones, Bloomberg, and Reuters News Service, as well as other required outlets. This is necessary because the wire services are highly competitive and each is as important as the other. Simultaneous release is the simplest and fairest way.
- *Distribution via PR Newswire or Business Newswire.* PR Newswire Associates, Inc. is a private organization with direct wires into every major financial publication in the United States, as well as the general wire services, general publications, and major brokerage houses. Business Newswire is the same kind of service, focusing primarily on business publications and brokerage firms. Both cover more than 2,000 brokerage houses and similar firms. There are also regional private wire services. Most wire services interface with others around the country.

It's the fastest and most efficient way to disseminate news. Distribution to Dow Jones, Bloomberg, and Reuters, as well as to all other appropriate publications, is covered by PR Newswire and Business Newswire. The release may be sent to the commercial wires by fax, phone, or hand delivered. It takes them about an hour to service the material and move it out on their wires. You may want to follow up with Dow Jones, Bloomberg, and Reuters, if the news is particularly sensitive, to explain any nuances or background. The commercial newswires will service local bureaus first. They usually service the Dow Jones, Bloomberg, and Reuters New York headquarters too, if you specify any New York distribution—which is important to know because it may conflict with your own primary distribution to those services.

- If the invitation to participate in a Webcast is broad enough to reach a substantive number of investors or potential investors, timely release by Webcast may qualify as timely disclosure. This is a call for an attorney.
- Depending upon the nature of the news, it's frequently a good idea to *hand deliver a copy of the release* to the business editor of the local newspaper, assuming that you've inquired first, by phone or e-mail, about his or her preferences for receiving information. Notify the local editor that there's a Dow Jones, Bloomberg or Reuters release or feature on your company. While the editor will ultimately receive the news from one of the wires, it's a courtesy that some editors appreciate.
- It's essential that news be distributed *early enough in the day* to warrant its being received by editors in the early morning for deadlines for the afternoon paper. The same is true of wire service distribution. Late releases may not make it through all the necessary distribution steps before market closing or by 5 PM, after which readership drops off considerably.
- In some cases, if you're known to the local editor, and you have more than run-of-the-mill news, it's not a bad idea to call by phone and alert the editor to the fact that the news is coming by wire or by hand. Considering the amount of news the editor must deal with on any given day, this call focuses attention on your news and can sometimes make the difference between its being printed or not. Issuing unfavorable earnings reports very late in the day, or managing not to be prepared to release them until Friday (for Saturday's paper), is bad practice. In the first place, it's illegal to hold any news of that nature for one minute

longer than is absolutely necessary for the broadest possible dissemination. Secondly, it fools no one. Bad news reverberates as urgently and as loudly as a firecracker in St. Patrick's Cathedral at high mass. And there are, of course, editors who will happily give a story that arrives in those circumstances more play than it would normally receive. For companies in trouble there is no place to hide.

Beyond meeting the needs of disclosure, there are now myriad ways of reaching the financial community beyond the wire services. Business Wire and others now serve the vast array of computer-accessed databases—CompuServe, DowPhone, NEXIS, Standard & Poor's and more. PR Newswire serves Bloomberg Financial Markets, which covers more than 5,000 brokerage firm terminals. A service called *First Call* is doing an excellent job of maintaining an active database (material stays active for 90 days) of information for brokerage firms, including analysts' reports. Many fax services will take your release or report to brokerage houses and distribute your one copy to hundreds of outlets at one time, although broadcast e-mail more frequently serves that purpose.

A word of caution about e-mail distribution to the press. As common or popular as it is, with a choice of receiving news by mail, fax, or e-mail, there are now few editors or reporters who don't make their preferences known. In fact preferences are now indicated in most media directories. These preferences should be respected.

Following the dissemination of the news to the wires and other appropriate media, the release should then be mailed or e-mailed to analysts, brokers, the trade media, shareholders (if appropriate), and any other interested parties. It's extremely important to distribute the release—by fax or hand for daily media and key market makers and investors, and by e-mail to others—even to those segments of the financial media and the financial community that might have received it over the Dow Jones, Bloomberg, or Reuters wires. First of all, it's unlikely that they will have carried the release in its entirely, even though the commercial Newswires will have done so. Second, there is no way to guarantee that the individual at either the publication or the Wall Street house you are interested in reaching will have seen it on the wire or have it on a terminal. Third, it gives a file copy to those individuals in both the financial community and in the media that are following the company. And fourth, it is one more opportunity to make the company name visible.

In this new era of electronic media, the traditional press release has lost is supremacy as a media relations tool. Fewer and fewer releases are being sent, in part because fewer and fewer releases are being read, but mostly because there are so many other ways for the media to get the news. And there is a growing tendency to want the short, curt, to-the-point message, telling the reporter enough to know whether he or she wants to follow up on the story. "Why wade through all the boilerplate," says one reporter. "I get the message quickly, and decide what I want to do with it." Moreover, the quality of the traditional press release has been deteriorating for years, and has been abused by its indiscriminate use. A two page release announcing to the major business media the appointment of new assistant treasurer will guarantee that the next release about the fire in plant number four will quickly be deleted or deep-sixed.

Print releases should be written, if written they must be, by people who are experienced in release writing, or who otherwise have journalistic skill. Unfortunately, since most financial releases are issued under the Rules of Disclosure, they are too often written by lawyers. Lawyers—even the most literate—should not be allowed to write final drafts of releases, including electronic releases. With rare exceptions, they tend to confuse releases with contracts, out of fear of being misinterpreted, misconstrued, or any of the other things lawyers worry about.

This is not to say that lawyers shouldn't assist in writing releases, or that releases shouldn't be cleared by lawyers when appropriate. Financial releases can have legal consequences, and it is this potential for trouble that should be reviewed by a lawyer. But the lawyer's purview is not literary style. It is fact and law, and the possibility of misinterpretation of facts as stated.

And which is not to say that a good lawyer can't be helpful in writing a release, if he understands the investor relations and media process, and will cooperate rather than attempt to dominate the release writing process.

Except under extreme circumstances, it's bad form to call an editor to find out why your release wasn't used. The chances are that it wasn't run because the editor didn't think it was important enough to print in his limited space or time, in relation to other information received that day. No medium is legally required to report any news, no matter how important it is to the company, and pestering an editor will only incur animosity and risk that subsequent releases will find their way directly to the wastebasket. If you do have something special, it is, however, appropriate to phone ahead, talk to the particular editor, advise him or her that the release is on the way, and that it addresses some noteworthy points. In view of the large number of releases received every day, if the news is important enough the editor will appreciate it and watch for it. It will not guarantee that it will be printed. There are times when it seems obvious that a release should have been printed and wasn't. It would be surprising, for example, if the earnings report of a major company in the apparel industry were not published by *Women's Wear Daily*. Under these circumstances, it's appropriate to phone the editor—not to ask why the release wasn't printed—but merely to confirm that the release was received. This is a subtle difference and frequently the publication will appreciate it if the editor has reason to believe that news he should have received never reached him.

In this context, it should be noted that the media sometimes makes mistakes. Releases do get lost. A paper will print the wrong number, or the broadcaster will get a fact wrong. Corrections become a problem, particularly if the error is minor (and certainly if its the fault of the issuer, and not the media).

When your story is one of hundreds received, and not run, with only dozens run that day, it's not likely to be of great concern to the publication unless it's a serious mistake, and you might be wasting your time—and risking the animus of the media—to make a fuss about it. If it's a consequential mistake, you're likely to get a rational response to a quiet (but not angry) presentation of the facts. The wire services particularly dislike taking up wire time with corrections, and Dow Jones can be made very happy by being told, "Look...don't worry about the wire, but get it straight in the paper." That's terrific—the record is in the paper, and the e-mail you sent out to the data services will cover those records. But everybody's human, and everybody makes honest mistakes, and everybody does his best to correct them. Both Reuters and Dow Jones will correct mistakes if they think the correction is important, but the sooner after publication that the mistake is noted, the easier to get a correction.

MAJOR NEWS COVERAGE

Major news can sometimes be treated somewhat differently than routine releases. If the news is of sufficient consequence to warrant greater attention than just routine dissemination, there are other techniques that can be used.

Remember, too, that today's business media is more involved in the companies it covers that it was in the past. Reporters, particularly those from major business media, feel that they are entitled to direct access to the CEO, CFO, chairman of the board, and other company executives. They don't hesitate to call directly, circumventing the investor relations officer or communications department. The warning here, of course, is to be sure that your company's executives are prepared, and that there is a press policy in place.

THE INDIVIDUAL INTERVIEW

There are times when the most effective way to break a major story is to give it to a single reporter in an exclusive interview. The strategy for this approach can be very subtle, such as an implied trade of major coverage in exchange for the exclusive, or when the reporter is important in his or her own right, as a columnist or well-known broadcaster might be. It's sometimes valuable, as well, when the story is somewhat technical, and requires a knowledgeable and concerned reporter for accurate coverage.

This may be effective, but it has an inherent danger. If there is any information imparted that comes under the Rules of Disclosure, that reporter's lead time and exclusivity may be lost, since the rules may require that the story be distributed to the general public within a reasonable period of time—and certainly the same day—as it is released to an individual. This is a matter to be discussed with the company's attorney. An exception is a *Wall Street Journal* or Reuters interview, which is accepted by the SEC as having broad enough coverage to be considered adequate under the rules of disclosure. In any event, any material information disclosed must immediately be disseminated.

BASIC INTERVIEW GUIDELINES

Here, too, the general guidelines for the interview are the same as for the media conference—careful preparation, no nonsense, to the point, and frank discussion.

In both the individual interview and the media conference there are two basic cautions to consider:

- *Be prepared for full disclosure.* Beware any question on a material matter a reporter might ask that you can't answer. If you can't answer because you don't know, say so—but be prepared to explain why you don't know. Promise to get the information and forward it on a timely basis. If a reporter feels you have anything to hide, his story based on the interview may nullify much or all of the positive effect that the story might otherwise have. Certainly, as in an analyst meeting, all possible questions should be anticipated and the answers prepared beforehand. Obviously, it's impossible to anticipate every question, and if an unanticipated question is asked, don't answer hastily, without considering how your words will look in type and material questions should be anticipated. There should be no surprises, if they can be avoided. Regulation FD applies here.

- At the same time, no matter how open you're willing to be, there may be questions that you shouldn't answer, for competitive or strategic reasons. Decline to answer those questions, but again, state the reasons. Again, these are questions that should be anticipated, and for which responses should be rehearsed.

- *Absolutely nothing should be stated off the record,* unless its pertinence to the story is for background only. An off-the-record statement places an unwarranted burden on a reporter. The reporter's job is to print information—not to be a repository of unusable facts. It is a burden that reporters rarely appreciate. Furthermore, it almost invariably leads to the impression that something else is being hidden. If you don't want a reporter to report something, don't say it—on or off the record. On the other hand, don't confuse *off the record* with *not for attribution,* which means that the material can be used, but please, the reporter shouldn't quote you on it. Know the difference, and follow the rules.

THE NEWS CONFERENCE

News people are too busy to spend several hours away from their desks to attend a news conference. They get particularly disturbed—and appropriately so—if they are invited to a news conference and are led to believe that they will be given news of greater importance than it is actually is. The fact that they are wined and dined is not of the essence. There is no law that says that a reporter who accepts your hospitality has to print your story. Media people are further annoyed by being invited to a news conference to be given news that can just as easily be covered by an e-mail or even a telephone interview.

A news conference should be called only when...

- The news is monumental.
- There is some clear reason—such as a complex and important merger or reorganization, demonstration of a new product that needs an elaborate explanation or demonstration—that can't easily be explained in a media release.
- Full understanding of the news requires questioning and elaborate answers.

FEATURE MATERIAL

The approach to developing feature material in business and financial publications, as well as the general media, is considerably different than it is for the straight news announcement. The attempt, in developing features, is to project a somewhat detailed and rounded picture of the company or some aspect of it, and to do so in a favorable way. The value of feature articles about a company lies not only in the general exposure of the company to the publication's readers, but in explaining the company with some measure of depth; to engender the impression that it's functioning well; and to increase the understanding of the company.

An article about Bill Gates, the head of Microsoft, that deals with his extensive and impressive charities, tells a great deal about the manager as an individual and a personality. The feature article, then, may deal with the personality or idiosyncrasies of its managers, or the work of its research department, or its unique approach to using raw materials. It doesn't matter which approach is used—it tells more about the company than do the numbers.

GUIDELINES FOR FEATURE ARTICLES

In approaching this kind of media coverage there are several basic rules and guidelines that are imperative. These rules apply whether the story is generated internally by the company or by the investor relations or public relations consultant.

- *The target media must be clearly understood.* Several issues of the publication or of the broadcast programs should be studied to determine the kind of material it seeks, its point of view, its style, its editorial viewpoint, and its apparent taboos. Any attempt to try to convince a medium to run a story that is not in keeping with its general editorial policy, or that's similar to one recently run, is not only a waste of time, but could lead to adverse reaction by the editors to the company or the investor relations consultant.

- *Even a feature article must have a newsworthy point of view.* Sometimes this is a *hook*—an event or activity that serves as a focal point for the story; an indication that the timing for the story is appropriate. Or it can be an angle that is at least unusual and perhaps unique, such as a company's new approach to financing or a new production or distribution technique that should result in significantly altering the direction of the company. Or the reorganization of a management team to take into account the changing economic conditions under which the company must function.
- The story should delineate, in one aspect or another, a *significant change in the company's operation.* It is only under the rarest circumstances that a publication will publish a story about a company in which absolutely nothing significant has happened, or in which the company is shown to be no different than any other company in its field. An exception might be when lack of change is significant and salutary in itself, such as when every other company in the industry has made significant changes with unfavorable results and the subject company, by changing nothing, has outperformed the industry.

DEVELOPING FEATURE MATERIAL ANGLES

Developing feature material for publication usually requires a measure of skill, if not artfulness. Some time ago, as part of its investor relations program, it was deemed valuable to develop a feature article about a medium-sized insurance company. Basic investigation indicated that the company's operations seemed no different than comparable companies in its industry. Furthermore, an additional obstacle existed in that newspapers infrequently find most stories of insurance companies of sufficient consequence to print. Every aspect of the company's business was carefully explored in the attempt to fathom some point that was unusual and newsworthy. There came to light the fact that the company's return on its investment portfolio was higher than most other insurance companies', including some of the giants. Further investigation showed that this was a function of the investment department's imagination and daring. It was company policy to seek out unusual situations, perhaps with somewhat more risk, and to be considerably more venturesome than is traditionally expected of the insurance industry. The company, for example, was one of the first to invest in the cable television industry.

This extraordinary success in portfolio management became the focal point of a proposal to the *New York Times,* which resulted in a large feature story on page one of the Sunday *New York Times* business section.

When a kid rescues another kid from drowning, it takes no public relations skill to get the kids' names in the paper. The skill is in fathoming the unusual but accurate in an otherwise usual story, and projecting it as the basis for a feature article.

APPROACHING A PUBLICATION

Approaching the media requires some relatively simple procedures...

- Once a *target medium* has been selected and its editorial policies analyzed, develop the story specifically for that medium. The same general story may function for several different publications, but each approach must still be tailored.
- *The proper reporter or editor* is determined either by reading the masthead, reading the publication or viewing the program, checking media directories, or by calling the publication and inquiring. In most major business publications, reporters can initiate stories, without assignment from an editor. In some publications, such as the *Wall Street Journal,* the *New York Times, Business Week* or *Fortune,* there are specific areas of specialty. In a smaller publication, the ranking editor on the masthead is the first point of contact. In larger magazines, such as Fortune, several people are given the specific responsibility for reviewing all story ideas. If there is a local bureau of the publication in or near your city, you will probably be better off working with it, rather than with the publication's national staff. This is particularly true of *Business Week* and the *Wall Street Journal.* (However, being turned down by a local bureau doesn't preclude going to the head office of a publication, if you're sure that's the right publication for the story, and the local bureau is informed of what you're doing.) In some cases, if you know a staff reporter but want to pitch to an editor, you

can call the reporter for advice about who to send the story to—but don't abuse this privilege.

- E-mail or write a letter to the editor or reporter describing the story. In some cases the letter may be preceded by a phone call or even a meeting with the editor. Experience and the media directories will tell you who prefers letters, who will take phone calls first, and who will take faxes or e-mails. Almost invariably, and with very few exceptions, the story may ultimately have to be presented to the publication in written form. Sometimes the presentation can be prepared before the first contact. Sometimes, if a discussion with the editor beforehand is feasible, the presentation should be written only after the meeting, and should be patterned on the guidelines set forth by the editor. If the phone call came first, the letter or e-mail should follow within one day.

  The presentation should be concise and to the point. The editor is busy and businesslike, and even the fact that he or she has been bought a sumptuous lunch at an expensive restaurant is not going to preclude the necessity he faces to maintain the level of his publication. The essence of the story should be stated in the first paragraph, with emphasis on the reasons why this story is newsworthy and warrants his consideration. The remainder of the brief letter should include facts to support the basic premise. It should indicate the availability of the people involved, and of graphic and visual material, if appropriate, that is available or can be made available to supplement the story.

  If you feel that the story is too long and complicated to cover in one page, consider using an outline, as long as you can still make it sound interesting. The letter should rarely be more than two pages long.

- The course of all interviews should take precisely the same form as interviews for major news events, and should follow the same rules described earlier in this chapter. The executives involved should be prepared to be frank and open. Nothing should be off the record except material that is necessary for background, but not necessarily newsworthy in itself. Questions should be anticipated and careful preparation made for each answer.

  Sometimes, (but not always) an interviewee can control an interview to some extent. First, you should have a clear idea of what you want the results to be, in terms of tone and information imparted. Then, with careful rehearsal, you can assure that the information comes out by being responsive to questions, and then going beyond the answer. For example...

Q. Do you think you'll make more acquisitions?

A. It's not in our immediate plans. However, we didn't plan to make the last acquisition, but the opportunity came up and we took it, because we always look at every opportunity in terms of our long range needs. That, to us, is as much a part of our planning as a dedicated acquisition program, because the aim is growth and diversification—not acquisition. We do, however, have the financial resources to take advantage of such opportunities.

In the case of smaller newspapers, or papers in other than the ten largest cities in the United States, the letter may ultimately turn out to be unnecessary. Arrangements can be made by phone. If an executive is planning to be in Birmingham, Alabama, next Thursday and there is reason to believe that there is a newsworthy aspect to either his presence in that city or to his company, it is perfectly appropriate to phone the financial editor of the Birmingham News a few days ahead, to indicate the fact that the executive will be in Birmingham next Thursday and to go on to delineate the basic points of the story in exactly the same way as is done in the letter. Be sure to point out a local angle to the company that might interest readers. Arrangements for the interview are then made by phone. Because unanticipated assignments may change plans, last minute confirmation is prudent. Obviously, more lead time than a few days affords a better chance for success, but that shouldn't preclude at least a try on a few days notice when that's all you've got.

In some cases an executive may be appearing in a city for purposes other than strictly company business. For example, the company president may be appearing in town to make a speech before a local organization. The procedure is to phone ahead to the editor and inform him of that fact. If the editor is not short-staffed and can afford time for coverage of the event, arrangements should be made. If possible, prepared material should be made available to the editor at the time of the interview. If the story is still considered newsworthy, but the editor is unable to assign a reporter to cover it, it is worth the effort to prepare a news release covering the event and to hand deliver or fax it to the editor on that morning.

OTHER MEDIA OPPORTUNITIES

Other media opportunities offer interesting possibilities.

A number of publications that include *Barron's* and *Fortune, Investor's Daily,* and *The Security Trader's Handbook,* reprint media releases in a special section for a small fee. This is particularly useful for the smaller company that is not likely to get wide media coverage for its routine news. While this kind of service might well be construed as advertising, it can be useful in hitting a well-defined target audience.

Not to be overlooked is the trade media. Articles and interviews, as well as media releases with financial information, frequently find hospitality in the industry trade media for a company. Analysts read the trade papers of industries or companies they follow. People in an industry are investors as well as are readers of the daily media, and there are good marketing reasons for a company to be seen in its industry's media. The rules for dealing with the trade media, incidentally, are no different than they are for dealing with the financial media.

THE UNEXPECTED INQUIRY

A reporter may hear a rumor, or have an intuitive thought, or otherwise draw a conclusion about a company—and call the CEO to follow it up. Whether the call is hostile or friendly, it's frequently unexpected.

The unexpected inquiry should also be dealt with in a straightforward manner. Remember, an officer of a public company has a fiduciary position. This means that public comment may have legal implications. This should be kept in mind in every aspect of dealing with the media, including the electronic media. Again, Regulation FD applies.

In responding to an inquiry, no attempt should be made to hide or dissemble—it will only make matters worse. The company CEO who is called by a reporter or an editor and asked to comment on an unfavorable rumor should react calmly and rationally. Always be aware that any material information that might fall under Regulation FD must be disclosed broadly immediately following the interview. If the facts are clearly at hand, he or she should state them simply and straightforwardly, with no obvious attempt to influence the editorial stance. If the CEO doesn't know the answer he should say so, take the reporter's name and phone number, get the information as soon as possible, and return the call with the facts. If warranted, the CEO should invite the reporter to discuss the question in detail, and here too the same rules apply as for any other interview. It's absolutely imperative that every company have a basic news policy. Specific executives should be designated as spokesmen for the company. The corps of spokesmen can be broad, consisting of specialists in each field, but they should not be arbitrarily selected, and each should be capable of dealing with the media calmly and intelligently.

There should be a clear and simple directive from the chief executive officer to all executives and employees that spokespersons have been designated and that all inquiries should be referred to the appropriate spokesperson. Under no circumstances should an unauthorized person be allowed to supply vital information to the media, and this should be made clear not in terms of authority alone, but rather for the simple reason that only the spokesmen have all pertinent facts and policy at hand. It should be made clear that it is as unfair to an unauthorized person to allow him or her to supply information as it is to the company, since it puts the unauthorized person in an untenable position. Unauthorized personnel should be advised to deal with all inquiries politely, to indicate that they are not sufficiently armed with the facts to answer the question, and then to indicate the name and phone number of the designated spokesman.

Designated spokespeople should be kept abreast at all times of company news policy and procedures. They should be briefed as well as possible on all potential inquiries and the appropriate answers. They should know company policy and the limits of the information they are authorized to divulge. They should be made to understand clearly the basic procedures for answering inquiries in terms of dealing with reporters politely, rationally, unemotionally, and openly. When a question exceeds the limits of a spokesman's authority, he should politely say so and refer the reporter to the proper executive to handle that inquiry. All inquiries and the answers given should be made known—preferably in writing—as soon as possible to the chief executive officer.

THE CRISIS PRESS CALL

What do you do when the press calls with an inquiry about bad news?

Or when a reporter calls to tell you he's heard that the tanks holding oil reserves you've been carrying on your books as an asset are really empty? Or that the U.S. Justice Department has just found an off-shore bank account in your CFO's name containing millions of dollars? Or that your accounting firm has been complicitous in your treasurer's fraudulent bookkeeping, and that he's implicated you as part of the scheme?

While the inquiry may come as a surprise, especially if the accusation is false, the well-prepared company should have a plan in place for dealing with such calls.

Richard S. Levick, an attorney who heads Washington-based *Levick Strategic Communications,* the leading public relations firm for lawyers and other professionals, offers the following sound advice to lawyers. So sound is the advice that it applies to all corporate management...

- *Confront Bad News.* Imagine a partner coming to your office for advice after receiving the following voice-mail: "We understand your client's tire inflator product occasionally blows up and decapitates its user. Where should the film crew meet you in two days?" The situation was further complicated by the fact that the market-leading manufacturer was about to be purchased by a Fortune 500 company. The press, with its unfounded allegations, would kill the deal.

  When a litigation partner from a major law firm received just such a message, he chose to tackle the problem head-on. Even before he called the client, he first contacted his media consultant and they devised the initial strategy. Then the lawyer called the client, which meant the lawyer was able to present the client with both the problem and the solution.

  Next, the litigation public relations specialist immediately contacted the television producer and offered to cooperate (rather than ignore the problem). The offer to cooperate enticed the producer to agree to provide the interview questions in advance, a fairly rare but not unheard-of occurrence. With the questions in hand, the litigator and client were able to rebut each question with facts. Because they were responding in a calm, cooperative atmosphere, it became apparent that, while a tire inflator product was known to blow up with incorrect use, no such incident was known to have ever included the client's product. In fact, it emerged that the tragic incidences were much more likely tied to a competitive product. The willingness to deal directly with the producer created trust. And from that trust grew the cooperation that ultimately killed the story.

  All too often, because lawyers do not have relationships with litigation public relations experts, they lose precious time after a crisis first occurs. The most important developments in terms of media coverage occur within hours and sometimes minutes after the initial call. If you are hunting down your litigation public relations team at this point, you have already forfeited options.

- *The Truth Shall Set You Free.* After a partner was convicted a few years ago for fraud and money laundering, the managing partner of a large law firm became its spokesperson. In so doing, he took the opposite tack from most law firms, which prefer to hide and hope the story will go away. Next, he took full responsibility, thus sending a signal to his internal audience that the firm would survive the problem, and, to the external audience, that leadership was engaged. Finally, he sent a clear and credible message which said, "If this can happen here, where we are terrifically vigilant, it can happen anywhere. This is all about the problems that arise when organizations are, perforce, growing by leaps and bounds. We all need to be even more vigilant." The message had one huge advantage: it was true. The managing partner won so much respect from the media that, after the initial bad news day, legal publications ran stories flattering to the firm for its honesty and thoughtfulness.

- *Create a Different Story.* When a major international law firm elected to close its London office in the midst of broad UK expansion by American law firms, concern was raised that it would become the media's favorite example of an American law firm unable to hold its own in a highly competitive market.

    Conceding that they would suffer a bad news day in the London press, the firm's managing partner decided on a strategy that changed the story altogether. Immediately after closing the London office (for all the right reasons), the law firm became the sole U.S. sponsor of First Tuesday, a European-based high-profile series of networking meetings for venture capitalists and dot com executives. The ensuing landslide of positive press over the next year positioned the law firm as a tech-savvy firm, and overshadowed the memory of the London office closing.

- *The Positive Angle.* When a top partner decided to leave a major law firm, the firm feared the negative press that often accompanies the departure of high-profile partners. Recognizing that the departing lawyer had strong positive feelings about the firm, they asked him to contribute helpful comments to his new firm's press release. The resultant press release mentioned the firm in its second paragraph—and made it abundantly clear that the departure had everything to do with the lawyer wanting to work at a very large firm, and nothing whatsoever to do with any imputed deficiencies in his former firm.

- *No Such Thing as a Local Paper.* When a partner at a San Francisco law firm was accused of sexual harassment in a local tabloid, the law firm elected to ignore the allegations and deflect the story by telling enquiring minds to consider the source. They did, and soon the story started appearing in mainstream business newspapers and the legal press. The story took on a life of its own and the law firm looked negligent for ignoring the public warning signs. The lesson is that there is no such thing as a local paper. All publications, even on the internet, have varying degrees of relevancy. The good news about an over-communicative environment is that non-major publications provide fair warning of what is likely to come. Ignore them at your peril.

- *Always Market.* In the early 1990's critics claimed that a venerable law firm was outdated and soon to go out of business. Within three years it became the third fastest growing law firm on the East Coast. In 2002, critics applied the same reasoning to another major law firm, claiming its focus on technology and overly aggressive advertising had put the firm in danger. If it continues to be the forward-thinking firm that it has been for the past five years, the firm will survive and prosper—despite its current troubles—just as the East Coast firm did. In each case, the firm does not shy away from marketing and media because it receives some negative coverage. Instead, they knuckle down and consider how they can be more forward thinking and more committed to the long term, marketing all the while.

What Mr. Levick clearly demonstrates is that the skills of media relations can be complex, except in the hands of an experienced professional, trained and practiced in imaginative and innovative solutions to problems beyond the realm of most executives.

WHEN TO SAY NO

But are there ever times to tell the media to bug off, and leave you alone? Maybe.

If you're dealing with a hostile reporter or publication, and believe you're in a no-win situation, you may have more to gain than to lose by refusing to cooperate.

If you're dealing with a publication whose editor thinks it's more important than it really is, and you know you're not going to get a fair shake anyway, why waste your time?

If you're asked to comment about a competitor, or about a situation in your industry to which you're ancillary, and there's a good chance that your comment may be misinterpreted or even misreported, "no comment" is a great response.

If you know that you're going to take a beating no matter what you say or do, or if you know that the reporter is unlettered or unknowledgeable in the subject and is only passing through the beat, or if you know that commenting is going to get you involved in something that may turn out to be unprofitable to you, then tell the media, politely, that you choose not to participate.

If you know that a reporter is misrepresenting to you what he's writing, in order to get your participation in a story that you might otherwise be reticent about, or if that reporter has done that to you in the past, you're perfectly right to decline.

In fact, participating in a roundup story should be done cautiously anyway, with you asking the reporter as many questions as he or she asks you. And if you do consider participating, take notes of what you're being told about the nature of the story. You may want to complain later.

The media has an inalienable right to pursue. They don't have an inalienable right to catch. There's a difference between being firm in declining and being rude. Rudeness is somebody else's game. Declining firmly and politely may very well be the way for you to win your game.

Except in terms of their training, and the motivation of individuals to do their jobs as well as possible, media people are no different from anybody else. The range of the capabilities, understanding, and limitations is about on a par with the total population. There are competent journalists and there are incompetent journalists. There are a great many reporters in the financial media who seem remarkably ignorant of business and finance. There are a greater number who are remarkably well versed in the field. Editors and newspapermen are no more exempt from hostilities, bad days, fights with their spouses, and toothaches than anybody else. Nevertheless, if they are dealt with professionally they will normally function professionally.

The editor and the journalists usually have no ax to grind. The realities of the world are that they react as humanly to a confrontation as does anyone else. Few journalists, however, will react unfavorably to an honest, simple, and straightforward presentation and to an unflinching response to even the most cutting questions.

The proper function of an investor relations consultant in dealing with the media is not to act as a spokesman for the company—unless he or she has been properly trained and specifically designated in this capacity by the chief executive officer—but to act as an intermediary, smoothing the way for direct relations between the company and the media. Nor should the investor relations consultant ever be used as a buffer—as a shield behind which the company can hide. The media resents this and rightfully so. Yet the major source of company news is still the investor relations consultant or officer.

And it's clearly acceptable to the media that the investor relations professional can be an advocate for the company he or she represents. A senior *Fortune* editor has said that she understands that a public relations or investor relations professional is fulfilling an advocacy function when talking about a client or employer. A *Wall Street Journal* reporter who sometimes writes the *Heard On The Street* column sees it from a different angle, saying, "I assume that everyone who gives me a positive story idea is long in the stock, and that everyone who gives me a negative idea is short." At least some reporters are aware of the sometimes unscrupulous use of the media by shorts.

Still, if there were no investor relations industry, every editorial body in the United States would have to treble its staff to ferret out the massive amount of news that is now brought to the attention of the media. Most journalists recognize this. Some journalists, however, given reason to feel that the investor relations professional is inserting himself or herself between the company and the media, will rightfully and vocally resent it.

The print and electronic media, when properly dealt with, are an important conduit to the financial community and the investing public. It's worth the effort of every corporate executive to learn to work with the media properly and effectively. Good media relations serves to characterize the company—to give it dimension beyond numbers. When done well, it enhances credibility, and most significantly demonstrates managements' skills.

CHAPTER 8

The Future of Investor Relations

If We Don't Know Where We're Going, How Do We Know How to Get There?

Predicting the future of anything is, as the British say, a mug's game. We can assume that the future is merely a singular and lineal projection of what is now, but we know better. We can guess, but only know for sure that our best guess will be knocked out by a random, unpredictable event, or a complex series of events.

Still, it seems important to try to fathom what comes next, so that we have a sense of what to do now to be prepared for the future. Well, if not a sense, then perhaps a whiff. To think that any of us can divine the future with anything but a lucky guess is to accept the same kind of hubris that led to the corporate and accounting disasters of the past several years.

In 2003, The American Assembly of Columbia University gathered to assess the future of the accounting profession. Great minds labored at it, and major figures addressed it. But in the end, they decided only that the present has to change. Oh. Being a seer is a cumbersome business.

Historians look at change from a larger perspective, and tend to see how changes create new social orders. In business history, for example, they see the birth pangs of the joint stock company. Could they have seen, in earlier times, the role the joint stock company—the modern corporation—could have contributed to building a great nation? No record of that.

What, then, are the elements that will shape the future for the corporation and its investors? There are several, and they provide the framework for what Churchill called an enigma wrapped in a mystery.

There is first of all the economy itself. In reveling in a thriving economy, or in berating ourselves for a poor economy, we come to recognize that the economy is driven by forces mostly beyond our control. And too often, those who contribute to change are too often lacking in perspective, which means they don't help much. In fact, one of the charges hurled against Wall Street is that their perspective on the world goes all the way from the opening bell to the closing gong on any given day. Yes, there are things we can do and things we can't do to give leverage to the economy, but it's like a giant ship, with a large turning radius. Controlling the economy, beyond some tweaking, is beyond us.

Regulation leads to change. Even within the short time we've had Sarbanes-Oxley and Regulation FD, we've seen massive changes in corporate governance, in the board room and the board's relationship to management and the financial operation, in a company's relations with its shareholders.

Technology brought vast changes in every aspect of management, from communication to financial controls to operations in both the front office and the factory floor to the accounting world. In less than a decade, the ubiquitous IBM Selectric typewriter went from state-of-the-art to obsolete. Where international trading was once rare, and limited to an adventurous few, today it's as normal as buying stock in General Motors or Microsoft. If capital, as economists are wont to say, knows no borders, with internet technology, capital crosses borders with the speed of light. Where, for eons, the world was governed by the clock, today worldwide communications defy the clock.

And so we have globalization, in which borders virtually disappear. Despite dislocations caused by international competition and outsourcing jobs to lesser developed countries, virtually no business in America, no matter how small, is untouched by the products, the capital, the economies of other nations. The emergence of the European Economic Community, and the success of the universal currency—the Eurodollar—turns Europe into one single economic entity, with policies that have forceful impact on American companies. As for the dislocations, such as the loss of jobs through outsourcing, time and the economy seem to have ways to accommodate. Ultimately, the shift in employment configurations become part of our economy and we move forward, Small consolation to those whose jobs are lost, but the economy adjusts, just as it has with such events as the computerized factory and other such technological advances that made many human crafts obsolete. Economies, we should know by now, absorb major changes. It's inherent in our capitalist system and in our democracy.

One thing we do know is that the economy, especially one the size of the American economy, is an ecology. Change something here, and it causes changes there. For example, outsourcing jobs to India means loss of jobs here, but helps build the Indian economy, giving them the resources to buy the American equipment needed to perform the services outsourced to them. This helps to create new jobs here, although not necessarily jobs for the same people whose jobs were outsourced. Losing a job that's been outsourced is painful, but, as President John F. Kennedy once said, a rising tide lifts all boats. The timing may be tragic for some, made especially worse if the government is slow to recognize the pain of unemployment, but that's why governments change in a democracy.

As to the future of investor relations, looking at the past can sometimes help us understand how the future evolves, even if it doesn't predict the future accurately. A look at the first edition of this book, *Competing For Capital,* in 1977 shows us practices that today seem quaint. There was no internet, nor were there web sites. All company financial data was transmitted by mail. The printed quarterly report to shareholders was standard. The number of public companies was half what it is today. The 401(k) plan, in which a vast number of working people became investors, hadn't come into existence. And the practice of corporate dealings with the investment public was called *financial relations,* or *financial public relations.* The competition for capital seems ponderous in retrospect, and especially when compared to today's economy.

What changed all that—some of it slowly and by attrition and evolution, and some of it with startling speed—was a different economy, new and penetrating regulation, new corporate practices and new structures of corporate governance, globalization, and perhaps most abruptly and urgently, new technology. The very factors that will change investor relations practice in the future. These are the factors that will change our economic world in the future. These factors—plus the uniquely entrepreneurial spirit of America.

In the early days of investor relations—financial public relations, if you will—our major role was to sit outside the corporate board room, waiting for permission to issue the dividend release. We were public relations people, specializing in a company's financial dealings with the public. As the financial world changed, the investor relations practice changed to a financial function with public relations overtones. Now, the investor relations professional is exactly that—a professional, with a strong financial background, and a strong knowledge of the corporate and financial function.

If the next step is to bring investor relations and its practitioners into the board room, this is a natural progression that redounds to intelligent corporate management practice.

It's no accident that NIRI—the National Investor Relations Institute—contributes so much more to the practice than many other professional organizations. It's made up of people who are professional and knowledgeable. More than any other association that deals with communication, it educates its members, it influences legislation and regulation, it advances the state-of-the-art of investor relations, it successfully espouses the cause of it s members to the corporate and legislative world. Whatever the future of investor relations, NIRI will help shape it.

For all that and all that, the future of investor relations will be shaped by the dynamic configuration of the economy, of regulations, of corporate practice, of globalization, of technology. Pay attention. To know the future of investor relations, that dynamic is what you have to watch.

About the Author

Bruce W. Marcus is a widely published author and consultant who has practiced both investor relations and marketing for professionals for almost half a century. He ran his first security analyst's meeting in the late 1950s, and wrote his first book on investor relations—*Competing for Capital* (Wiley)—in 1975. This is the fourth update of that book. He has had his own investor relations firm, and was a senior officer of The Financial Relations Board. He is the author of hundreds of articles and more than a dozen books on investor relations, the capital markets, ERISA, marketing, marketing related subjects, and as the editor of *The Marcus Letter on Professional Services Marketing* (www.marcusletter.com)—one of the most widely read publications on the subject—he has been at the forefront of the changes and maturity of the art of professional services marketing and investor relations. As a marketing consultant, he has brought innovative marketing programs to both large and small professional firms. He is the co-author, most recently, of *Client at the Core— Marketing and Managing Today's Professional Firm* (Wiley). He can be reached at marcus@marcusletter.com.